50 Canadian Cake Flavor Recipes for Home

By: Kelly Johnson

Table of Contents

- Maple Pecan Cake
- Butter Tart Cake
- Nanaimo Bar Cake
- Lemon Blueberry Cake
- Cedar and Apple Cake
- Cranberry Orange Cake
- Pumpkin Spice Cake
- Saskatoon Berry Cake
- Maple Walnut Cake
- Peach Cobbler Cake
- Cherry Blossom Cake
- Molasses Spice Cake
- Rhubarb Almond Cake
- Hummingbird Cake
- Maple Bacon Cake
- Red Velvet Cake
- Prairie Berry Cake
- Victoria Sponge Cake
- Chocolate Avocado Cake
- Blueberry Lemon Buttermilk Cake
- Apple Cinnamon Cake
- Maple Cream Cheese Cake
- Almond Joy Cake
- Whiskey and Honey Cake
- Butterscotch Cake
- Pear and Ginger Cake
- Bumbleberry Cake
- Chocolate Mint Cake
- Coconut Pineapple Cake
- Strawberry Rhubarb Cake
- Dulce de Leche Cake
- Maple Apple Cake
- Pecan Pie Cake
- Mango Coconut Cake
- Lemon Lavender Cake
- Pumpkin Caramel Cake

- Maple Carrot Cake
- Raisin Spice Cake
- Coffee and Walnut Cake
- Lemon Raspberry Cake
- Blackberry Ginger Cake
- Poppy Seed Cake
- Maple Berry Bundt Cake
- Chocolate Chai Cake
- Fig and Walnut Cake
- Vanilla Bean Cake
- Huckleberry Cake
- Maple Bacon Caramel Cake
- Chocolate Cherry Cake
- Butternut Squash Cake

Maple Pecan Cake

Ingredients:

For the Cake:

- 1 1/2 cups (190g) all-purpose flour
- 1 1/2 teaspoons baking powder
- 1/2 teaspoon baking soda
- 1/4 teaspoon salt
- 1/2 cup (115g) unsalted butter, softened
- 1 cup (200g) granulated sugar
- 2 large eggs
- 1/2 cup (120ml) pure maple syrup
- 1/2 cup (120ml) buttermilk or sour cream
- 1 teaspoon vanilla extract
- 1/2 cup (60g) chopped pecans (toasted)

For the Maple Frosting:

- 1/2 cup (115g) unsalted butter, softened
- 1 1/2 cups (190g) powdered sugar
- 1/4 cup (60ml) pure maple syrup
- 1 tablespoon milk (or more, if needed)
- 1/2 teaspoon vanilla extract

For Garnish (optional):

- Whole pecans
- Drizzle of maple syrup

Instructions:

1. **Prepare the Cake:**
    - Preheat your oven to 350°F (175°C). Grease and flour an 8-inch (20cm) round cake pan or line it with parchment paper.
    - In a medium bowl, whisk together the flour, baking powder, baking soda, and salt.
    - In a large bowl, cream together the softened butter and granulated sugar until light and fluffy.
    - Beat in the eggs one at a time, mixing well after each addition. Stir in the maple syrup, buttermilk, and vanilla extract.
    - Gradually add the dry ingredients to the wet mixture, mixing until just combined.
    - Gently fold in the toasted pecans.
    - Pour the batter into the prepared cake pan and smooth the top with a spatula.
    - Bake for 30-35 minutes, or until a toothpick inserted into the center comes out clean and the cake is golden brown.

- Allow the cake to cool in the pan for 10 minutes, then transfer to a wire rack to cool completely.

2. **Prepare the Maple Frosting:**
   - In a medium bowl, beat the softened butter until creamy.
   - Gradually add the powdered sugar, beating well after each addition.
   - Add the maple syrup, milk, and vanilla extract, and continue to beat until smooth and spreadable. Adjust the consistency with more milk if needed.
3. **Assemble the Cake:**
   - Once the cake is completely cooled, frost the top and sides with the maple frosting.
   - Garnish with whole pecans and a drizzle of maple syrup, if desired.
4. **Serve:**
   - Slice and serve the cake at room temperature. It pairs wonderfully with a cup of coffee or tea.

Tips:

- **Toasting Pecans:** Toast the pecans in a dry skillet over medium heat for about 5 minutes, stirring frequently, until fragrant and lightly browned. Let them cool before adding to the batter.
- **Maple Syrup:** Use pure maple syrup for the best flavor. Avoid maple-flavored syrup as it contains artificial flavors and is not as rich.
- **Storage:** The cake can be stored in an airtight container at room temperature for up to 3 days or refrigerated for up to a week. It can also be frozen for up to 2 months; thaw in the refrigerator before serving.

Maple Pecan Cake is a delightful dessert that combines the richness of maple syrup with the crunch of toasted pecans, making it a perfect treat for any occasion!

Butter Tart Cake

Ingredients:

For the Cake:

- 1 1/2 cups (190g) all-purpose flour
- 1 1/2 teaspoons baking powder
- 1/4 teaspoon salt
- 1/2 cup (115g) unsalted butter, softened
- 1 cup (200g) granulated sugar
- 2 large eggs
- 1/2 cup (120ml) whole milk
- 1/2 teaspoon vanilla extract

For the Butter Tart Filling:

- 1/2 cup (115g) unsalted butter
- 1 cup (200g) packed brown sugar
- 1/2 cup (120ml) corn syrup or maple syrup
- 2 large eggs
- 1 teaspoon vanilla extract
- 1/2 cup (70g) chopped pecans or walnuts (optional)
- 1/4 teaspoon salt

For the Glaze (optional):

- 1/2 cup (60g) powdered sugar
- 2 tablespoons milk or cream
- 1/2 teaspoon vanilla extract

Instructions:

1. **Prepare the Cake:**
    - Preheat your oven to 350°F (175°C). Grease and flour an 8-inch (20cm) round cake pan or line it with parchment paper.
    - In a medium bowl, whisk together the flour, baking powder, and salt.
    - In a large bowl, cream together the softened butter and granulated sugar until light and fluffy.
    - Beat in the eggs one at a time, mixing well after each addition. Stir in the milk and vanilla extract.
    - Gradually add the dry ingredients to the wet mixture, mixing until just combined.
    - Pour the batter into the prepared cake pan and smooth the top with a spatula.
2. **Prepare the Butter Tart Filling:**
    - In a saucepan over medium heat, melt the butter. Stir in the brown sugar and corn syrup (or maple syrup) until the mixture is smooth and well combined.

- Remove from heat and let it cool slightly. Whisk in the eggs, vanilla extract, and salt until the mixture is smooth. Stir in the chopped nuts if using.
- Pour the butter tart filling over the cake batter in the pan.

3. **Bake the Cake:**
   - Bake in the preheated oven for 40-45 minutes, or until the cake is set and the filling is bubbly and golden brown. A toothpick inserted into the center should come out with a few moist crumbs but not wet batter.
   - Allow the cake to cool in the pan for 10 minutes before transferring it to a wire rack to cool completely.
4. **Prepare the Glaze (optional):**
   - In a small bowl, whisk together the powdered sugar, milk or cream, and vanilla extract until smooth.
   - Drizzle the glaze over the cooled cake.
5. **Serve:**
   - Slice and serve the cake at room temperature. It pairs well with a cup of coffee or tea.

Tips:

- **Butter Tart Filling:** Ensure the filling is slightly cooled before adding to the batter to avoid curdling the eggs.
- **Nuts:** Chopped pecans or walnuts add a delightful crunch but can be omitted if desired.
- **Storage:** The cake can be stored in an airtight container at room temperature for up to 3 days or in the refrigerator for up to a week. It can also be frozen for up to 2 months; thaw in the refrigerator before serving.

Butter Tart Cake offers the rich, sweet flavors of a traditional butter tart in a cake form, making it a unique and indulgent treat perfect for special occasions or any time you want to enjoy a classic Canadian dessert.

Nanaimo Bar Cake

Ingredients:

For the Base Layer:

- 1 cup (100g) graham cracker crumbs
- 1/2 cup (50g) finely shredded coconut
- 1/2 cup (115g) unsalted butter, melted
- 1/4 cup (50g) granulated sugar

For the Custard Filling:

- 1/2 cup (115g) unsalted butter, softened
- 2 cups (250g) powdered sugar
- 2 tablespoons vanilla custard powder (or vanilla pudding mix)
- 2 tablespoons milk
- 1 teaspoon vanilla extract

For the Chocolate Topping:

- 1/2 cup (115g) unsalted butter
- 2 cups (340g) semi-sweet chocolate chips
- 1 tablespoon light corn syrup (optional, for extra shine)

Instructions:

1. **Prepare the Base Layer:**
   - Preheat your oven to 350°F (175°C). Grease and line an 8-inch (20cm) square baking pan with parchment paper, leaving some overhang for easy removal.
   - In a medium bowl, mix the graham cracker crumbs, shredded coconut, melted butter, and granulated sugar until well combined.
   - Press the mixture evenly into the bottom of the prepared pan to form a crust.
   - Bake for 10 minutes, then remove from the oven and let it cool while you prepare the custard layer.
2. **Prepare the Custard Filling:**
   - In a large bowl, beat the softened butter until creamy.
   - Gradually add the powdered sugar, beating well after each addition.
   - Add the custard powder, milk, and vanilla extract, and continue to beat until smooth and spreadable.
   - Spread the custard mixture evenly over the cooled base layer.
3. **Prepare the Chocolate Topping:**
   - In a medium saucepan, melt the butter over low heat.
   - Add the chocolate chips and stir until the chocolate is completely melted and smooth.
   - Stir in the corn syrup, if using, for added shine.

- Pour the chocolate mixture over the custard layer, spreading it evenly with a spatula.
4. **Chill and Serve:**
    - Refrigerate the cake for at least 2 hours or until the chocolate is set.
    - Once set, lift the cake out of the pan using the parchment paper overhang and cut into squares.

Tips:

- **Custard Powder:** Vanilla custard powder is key to achieving the classic Nanaimo bar flavor. If you can't find it, you can use vanilla pudding mix as a substitute.
- **Chocolate Topping:** For a smoother topping, ensure that you melt the chocolate and butter over low heat to avoid scorching.
- **Storage:** Store the Nanaimo Bar Cake in an airtight container in the refrigerator for up to a week. It can also be frozen for up to 2 months; thaw in the refrigerator before serving.

Nanaimo Bar Cake brings the beloved flavors of Nanaimo bars into a cake form, making it a delightful and indulgent treat for any occasion. Enjoy this sweet and satisfying dessert!

Lemon Blueberry Cake

Ingredients:

For the Cake:

- 1 1/2 cups (190g) all-purpose flour
- 1 1/2 teaspoons baking powder
- 1/4 teaspoon salt
- 1/2 cup (115g) unsalted butter, softened
- 1 cup (200g) granulated sugar
- 2 large eggs
- 1/2 cup (120ml) milk (whole or buttermilk)
- 1/4 cup (60ml) fresh lemon juice
- 1 tablespoon lemon zest (about 1 lemon)
- 1 teaspoon vanilla extract
- 1 cup (150g) fresh or frozen blueberries (do not thaw if frozen)

For the Lemon Glaze (optional):

- 1 cup (120g) powdered sugar
- 2-3 tablespoons fresh lemon juice

For Garnish (optional):

- Additional lemon zest
- Fresh blueberries

Instructions:

1. **Prepare the Cake:**
    - Preheat your oven to 350°F (175°C). Grease and flour an 8-inch (20cm) round cake pan or line it with parchment paper.
    - In a medium bowl, whisk together the flour, baking powder, and salt.
    - In a large bowl, cream together the softened butter and granulated sugar until light and fluffy.
    - Beat in the eggs one at a time, mixing well after each addition.
    - Stir in the lemon juice, lemon zest, and vanilla extract.
    - Gradually add the dry ingredients to the wet mixture, alternating with the milk, beginning and ending with the flour mixture. Mix until just combined.
    - Gently fold in the blueberries.
    - Pour the batter into the prepared cake pan and smooth the top with a spatula.
2. **Bake the Cake:**
    - Bake in the preheated oven for 30-35 minutes, or until a toothpick inserted into the center comes out clean and the cake is golden brown.

- Allow the cake to cool in the pan for 10 minutes, then transfer to a wire rack to cool completely.

3. **Prepare the Lemon Glaze (optional):**
    - In a small bowl, whisk together the powdered sugar and lemon juice until smooth. Adjust the consistency with more lemon juice or powdered sugar if needed.
    - Drizzle the glaze over the cooled cake.
4. **Garnish and Serve:**
    - Garnish with additional lemon zest and fresh blueberries if desired.
    - Slice and serve at room temperature or slightly chilled.

Tips:

- **Blueberries:** If using frozen blueberries, keep them frozen until you fold them into the batter to prevent them from bleeding into the cake. Tossing them in a bit of flour before adding can help prevent sinking.
- **Lemon Juice:** Fresh lemon juice and zest provide the best flavor. Avoid bottled lemon juice if possible.
- **Storage:** The cake can be stored in an airtight container at room temperature for up to 3 days or refrigerated for up to a week. It can also be frozen for up to 2 months; thaw in the refrigerator before serving.

Lemon Blueberry Cake is a refreshing and flavorful dessert that is perfect for any occasion, whether it's a casual get-together or a special celebration. Enjoy this burst of citrus and berry goodness!

Cedar and Apple Cake

Ingredients:

For the Cake:

- 1 1/2 cups (190g) all-purpose flour
- 1/2 cup (60g) almond flour or finely ground almonds
- 1 teaspoon baking powder
- 1/2 teaspoon baking soda
- 1/4 teaspoon salt
- 1/2 cup (115g) unsalted butter, softened
- 1 cup (200g) granulated sugar
- 2 large eggs
- 1/2 cup (120ml) buttermilk or plain yogurt
- 1/4 cup (60ml) pure maple syrup (optional for added sweetness)
- 1 teaspoon vanilla extract
- 1 tablespoon finely grated cedar wood (use food-grade cedar or cedar essence, or finely chopped cedar leaves)
- 1 large apple, peeled, cored, and finely diced

For the Apple Cinnamon Glaze (optional):

- 1/2 cup (60g) powdered sugar
- 1 tablespoon apple cider
- 1/4 teaspoon ground cinnamon

For Garnish (optional):

- Thin apple slices
- A sprinkle of cinnamon

Instructions:

1. **Prepare the Cake:**
    - Preheat your oven to 350°F (175°C). Grease and flour an 8-inch (20cm) round cake pan or line it with parchment paper.
    - In a medium bowl, whisk together the all-purpose flour, almond flour, baking powder, baking soda, and salt.
    - In a large bowl, cream together the softened butter and granulated sugar until light and fluffy.
    - Beat in the eggs one at a time, mixing well after each addition.
    - Stir in the buttermilk (or yogurt), maple syrup (if using), and vanilla extract.
    - Gradually add the dry ingredients to the wet mixture, mixing until just combined.
    - Gently fold in the grated cedar wood and diced apple.
    - Pour the batter into the prepared cake pan and smooth the top with a spatula.

2. **Bake the Cake:**
   - Bake in the preheated oven for 35-40 minutes, or until a toothpick inserted into the center comes out clean and the cake is golden brown.
   - Allow the cake to cool in the pan for 10 minutes, then transfer to a wire rack to cool completely.
3. **Prepare the Apple Cinnamon Glaze (optional):**
   - In a small bowl, whisk together the powdered sugar, apple cider, and ground cinnamon until smooth. Adjust the consistency with more apple cider or powdered sugar if needed.
   - Drizzle the glaze over the cooled cake.
4. **Garnish and Serve:**
   - Garnish with thin apple slices and a sprinkle of cinnamon if desired.
   - Slice and serve at room temperature.

Tips:

- **Cedar Wood:** Use food-grade cedar or a small amount of cedar essence. Make sure the cedar you use is safe for culinary use. If you're unsure, you can omit it or use a small amount of cedar leaves for flavor.
- **Apple:** Use a crisp apple variety like Granny Smith or Honeycrisp for the best texture and flavor.
- **Storage:** The cake can be stored in an airtight container at room temperature for up to 3 days or refrigerated for up to a week. It can also be frozen for up to 2 months; thaw in the refrigerator before serving.

Cedar and Apple Cake is a unique and aromatic dessert that brings together the warmth of apple and the intriguing hint of cedar, creating a memorable treat for any occasion. Enjoy!

Cranberry Orange Cake

Ingredients:

For the Cake:

- 1 1/2 cups (190g) all-purpose flour
- 1 1/2 teaspoons baking powder
- 1/4 teaspoon baking soda
- 1/4 teaspoon salt
- 1/2 cup (115g) unsalted butter, softened
- 1 cup (200g) granulated sugar
- 2 large eggs
- 1/2 cup (120ml) buttermilk or plain yogurt
- 1/4 cup (60ml) fresh orange juice
- 1 tablespoon orange zest (about 1 orange)
- 1 cup (100g) fresh or frozen cranberries (do not thaw if frozen)
- 1 tablespoon all-purpose flour (for tossing cranberries)

For the Orange Glaze (optional):

- 1 cup (120g) powdered sugar
- 2-3 tablespoons fresh orange juice

For Garnish (optional):

- Fresh cranberries
- Orange zest

Instructions:

1. **Prepare the Cake:**
    - Preheat your oven to 350°F (175°C). Grease and flour an 8-inch (20cm) round cake pan or line it with parchment paper.
    - In a medium bowl, whisk together the flour, baking powder, baking soda, and salt.
    - In a large bowl, cream together the softened butter and granulated sugar until light and fluffy.
    - Beat in the eggs one at a time, mixing well after each addition.
    - Stir in the orange juice and orange zest.
    - Gradually add the dry ingredients to the wet mixture, alternating with the buttermilk (or yogurt), beginning and ending with the flour mixture. Mix until just combined.
    - Toss the cranberries with 1 tablespoon of flour to coat. Gently fold the cranberries into the batter.
    - Pour the batter into the prepared cake pan and smooth the top with a spatula.
2. **Bake the Cake:**

- Bake in the preheated oven for 30-35 minutes, or until a toothpick inserted into the center comes out clean and the cake is golden brown.
- Allow the cake to cool in the pan for 10 minutes, then transfer to a wire rack to cool completely.
3. **Prepare the Orange Glaze (optional):**
    - In a small bowl, whisk together the powdered sugar and orange juice until smooth. Adjust the consistency with more orange juice or powdered sugar if needed.
    - Drizzle the glaze over the cooled cake.
4. **Garnish and Serve:**
    - Garnish with fresh cranberries and additional orange zest if desired.
    - Slice and serve at room temperature.

Tips:

- **Cranberries:** Tossing the cranberries in flour helps prevent them from sinking to the bottom of the cake during baking.
- **Orange Juice:** Fresh orange juice provides the best flavor, but you can use bottled if necessary.
- **Storage:** The cake can be stored in an airtight container at room temperature for up to 3 days or in the refrigerator for up to a week. It can also be frozen for up to 2 months; thaw in the refrigerator before serving.

Cranberry Orange Cake is a delightful combination of sweet and tart flavors, making it a refreshing and delicious treat. Enjoy this vibrant cake with a cup of tea or as a festive dessert!

Pumpkin Spice Cake

Ingredients:

For the Cake:

- 1 1/2 cups (190g) all-purpose flour
- 1 1/2 teaspoons baking powder
- 1 teaspoon baking soda
- 1/2 teaspoon salt
- 2 teaspoons pumpkin pie spice (or a mix of ground cinnamon, nutmeg, ginger, and cloves)
- 1/2 cup (115g) unsalted butter, softened
- 1 cup (200g) granulated sugar
- 1/2 cup (100g) packed brown sugar
- 2 large eggs
- 1 cup (240ml) canned pumpkin (not pumpkin pie filling)
- 1/2 cup (120ml) buttermilk or milk
- 1 teaspoon vanilla extract

For the Cream Cheese Frosting:

- 1/2 cup (115g) unsalted butter, softened
- 8 oz (225g) cream cheese, softened
- 3-4 cups (375-500g) powdered sugar, sifted
- 1 teaspoon vanilla extract

For Garnish (optional):

- Ground cinnamon
- Chopped pecans or walnuts
- Pumpkin seeds

Instructions:

1. **Prepare the Cake:**
   - Preheat your oven to 350°F (175°C). Grease and flour an 8-inch (20cm) round cake pan or line it with parchment paper. You can also use two 8-inch round pans if you prefer a layered cake.
   - In a medium bowl, whisk together the flour, baking powder, baking soda, salt, and pumpkin pie spice.
   - In a large bowl, cream together the softened butter, granulated sugar, and brown sugar until light and fluffy.
   - Beat in the eggs one at a time, mixing well after each addition.
   - Stir in the canned pumpkin, buttermilk (or milk), and vanilla extract until well combined.

- Gradually add the dry ingredients to the wet mixture, mixing until just combined.
- Pour the batter into the prepared cake pan(s) and smooth the top with a spatula.
2. **Bake the Cake:**
    - Bake in the preheated oven for 30-35 minutes, or until a toothpick inserted into the center comes out clean and the cake is golden brown.
    - Allow the cake to cool in the pan for 10 minutes, then transfer to a wire rack to cool completely.
3. **Prepare the Cream Cheese Frosting:**
    - In a large bowl, beat the softened butter and cream cheese until creamy and smooth.
    - Gradually add the powdered sugar, beating well after each addition, until the frosting reaches your desired consistency.
    - Stir in the vanilla extract.
4. **Frost and Garnish:**
    - Once the cake is completely cooled, spread the cream cheese frosting evenly over the top and sides of the cake.
    - Garnish with a sprinkle of ground cinnamon, chopped pecans or walnuts, and pumpkin seeds if desired.
5. **Serve:**
    - Slice and serve the cake at room temperature. It pairs beautifully with a cup of coffee or tea.

Tips:

- **Pumpkin:** Use pure canned pumpkin for the best results. Avoid pumpkin pie filling as it contains added spices and sugar.
- **Spices:** Adjust the amount of pumpkin pie spice to your taste preference. You can use a combination of cinnamon, nutmeg, ginger, and cloves if you don't have pre-made pumpkin pie spice.
- **Storage:** The cake can be stored in an airtight container at room temperature for up to 3 days or refrigerated for up to a week. It can also be frozen for up to 2 months; thaw in the refrigerator before serving.

Pumpkin Spice Cake is a comforting and flavorful treat that captures the essence of fall. Enjoy the warm spices and creamy frosting with every bite!

Saskatoon Berry Cake

Ingredients:

For the Cake:

- 1 1/2 cups (190g) all-purpose flour
- 1 1/2 teaspoons baking powder
- 1/2 teaspoon baking soda
- 1/4 teaspoon salt
- 1/2 cup (115g) unsalted butter, softened
- 1 cup (200g) granulated sugar
- 2 large eggs
- 1/2 cup (120ml) sour cream or plain yogurt
- 1/4 cup (60ml) milk
- 1 teaspoon vanilla extract
- 1 1/2 cups (225g) fresh or frozen Saskatoon berries (do not thaw if frozen)
- 1 tablespoon all-purpose flour (for tossing berries)

For the Saskatoon Berry Compote (optional):

- 1 cup (150g) Saskatoon berries
- 1/4 cup (50g) granulated sugar
- 1 tablespoon lemon juice
- 1 tablespoon water

For the Glaze (optional):

- 1 cup (120g) powdered sugar
- 2-3 tablespoons lemon juice

For Garnish (optional):

- Fresh Saskatoon berries
- Lemon zest

Instructions:

1. **Prepare the Cake:**
    - Preheat your oven to 350°F (175°C). Grease and flour an 8-inch (20cm) round cake pan or line it with parchment paper.
    - In a medium bowl, whisk together the flour, baking powder, baking soda, and salt.
    - In a large bowl, cream together the softened butter and granulated sugar until light and fluffy.
    - Beat in the eggs one at a time, mixing well after each addition.
    - Stir in the sour cream (or yogurt), milk, and vanilla extract.

- Gradually add the dry ingredients to the wet mixture, mixing until just combined.
- Toss the Saskatoon berries with 1 tablespoon of flour to coat. Gently fold the berries into the batter.
- Pour the batter into the prepared cake pan and smooth the top with a spatula.

2. **Bake the Cake:**
    - Bake in the preheated oven for 30-35 minutes, or until a toothpick inserted into the center comes out clean and the cake is golden brown.
    - Allow the cake to cool in the pan for 10 minutes, then transfer to a wire rack to cool completely.
3. **Prepare the Saskatoon Berry Compote (optional):**
    - In a small saucepan, combine the Saskatoon berries, granulated sugar, lemon juice, and water.
    - Cook over medium heat, stirring occasionally, until the berries break down and the mixture thickens, about 10-15 minutes.
    - Remove from heat and let cool. This compote can be used as a topping or filling for the cake.
4. **Prepare the Glaze (optional):**
    - In a small bowl, whisk together the powdered sugar and lemon juice until smooth. Adjust the consistency with more lemon juice or powdered sugar if needed.
    - Drizzle the glaze over the cooled cake.
5. **Garnish and Serve:**
    - Garnish with fresh Saskatoon berries and a sprinkle of lemon zest if desired.
    - Slice and serve at room temperature. The compote can be served on the side or spooned over individual slices.

Tips:

- **Saskatoon Berries:** If using frozen berries, do not thaw them before adding to the batter to prevent bleeding into the cake. Tossing them in flour helps to keep them suspended in the batter.
- **Compote:** The Saskatoon berry compote adds extra flavor and is great for topping the cake or serving alongside it.
- **Storage:** The cake can be stored in an airtight container at room temperature for up to 3 days or in the refrigerator for up to a week. It can also be frozen for up to 2 months; thaw in the refrigerator before serving.

Saskatoon Berry Cake offers a delightful combination of sweet and tart flavors, making it a special treat that highlights the unique taste of Saskatoon berries. Enjoy this cake with a cup of tea or coffee for a delicious and satisfying dessert!

Maple Walnut Cake

Ingredients:

For the Cake:

- 1 1/2 cups (190g) all-purpose flour
- 1 1/2 teaspoons baking powder
- 1/2 teaspoon baking soda
- 1/4 teaspoon salt
- 1/2 cup (115g) unsalted butter, softened
- 1 cup (200g) granulated sugar
- 1/2 cup (120ml) pure maple syrup
- 2 large eggs
- 1/2 cup (120ml) buttermilk or milk
- 1 teaspoon vanilla extract
- 1 cup (120g) chopped walnuts, toasted (see note below)

For the Maple Cream Cheese Frosting:

- 1/2 cup (115g) unsalted butter, softened
- 8 oz (225g) cream cheese, softened
- 1/4 cup (60ml) pure maple syrup
- 3-4 cups (375-500g) powdered sugar, sifted

For Garnish (optional):

- Additional toasted walnuts
- Maple syrup drizzle

Instructions:

1. **Prepare the Cake:**
   - Preheat your oven to 350°F (175°C). Grease and flour an 8-inch (20cm) round cake pan or line it with parchment paper. You can also use two 8-inch round pans if you prefer a layered cake.
   - In a medium bowl, whisk together the flour, baking powder, baking soda, and salt.
   - In a large bowl, cream together the softened butter and granulated sugar until light and fluffy.
   - Beat in the eggs one at a time, mixing well after each addition.
   - Stir in the maple syrup, mixing until well combined.
   - Gradually add the dry ingredients to the wet mixture, alternating with the buttermilk (or milk), beginning and ending with the flour mixture. Mix until just combined.
   - Gently fold in the toasted chopped walnuts.
   - Pour the batter into the prepared cake pan(s) and smooth the top with a spatula.

2. **Bake the Cake:**
   - Bake in the preheated oven for 30-35 minutes, or until a toothpick inserted into the center comes out clean and the cake is golden brown.
   - Allow the cake to cool in the pan for 10 minutes, then transfer to a wire rack to cool completely.
3. **Prepare the Maple Cream Cheese Frosting:**
   - In a large bowl, beat the softened butter and cream cheese until creamy and smooth.
   - Gradually add the powdered sugar, beating well after each addition, until the frosting reaches your desired consistency.
   - Mix in the maple syrup until fully incorporated.
4. **Frost and Garnish:**
   - Once the cake is completely cooled, spread the maple cream cheese frosting evenly over the top and sides of the cake.
   - Garnish with additional toasted walnuts and a drizzle of maple syrup if desired.
5. **Serve:**
   - Slice and serve at room temperature. The cake pairs beautifully with a cup of coffee or tea.

Tips:

- **Toasting Walnuts:** To toast walnuts, spread them in a single layer on a baking sheet and bake at 350°F (175°C) for about 8-10 minutes, or until they are fragrant and lightly browned. Let them cool before chopping.
- **Maple Syrup:** Use pure maple syrup for the best flavor. Avoid imitation maple syrup as it does not have the same rich taste.
- **Storage:** The cake can be stored in an airtight container at room temperature for up to 3 days or in the refrigerator for up to a week. It can also be frozen for up to 2 months; thaw in the refrigerator before serving.

Maple Walnut Cake is a wonderfully flavorful dessert that combines the sweet richness of maple syrup with the nutty crunch of walnuts. Enjoy this comforting cake as a special treat for any occasion!

Peach Cobbler Cake

Ingredients:

For the Cake:

- 1 1/2 cups (190g) all-purpose flour
- 1 1/2 teaspoons baking powder
- 1/2 teaspoon baking soda
- 1/4 teaspoon salt
- 1/2 cup (115g) unsalted butter, softened
- 1 cup (200g) granulated sugar
- 2 large eggs
- 1/2 cup (120ml) sour cream or plain yogurt
- 1/2 cup (120ml) milk
- 1 teaspoon vanilla extract
- 2 cups (300g) fresh peaches, peeled, pitted, and chopped (or use canned peaches, drained)

For the Topping:

- 1/2 cup (100g) granulated sugar
- 1/4 cup (30g) all-purpose flour
- 1/2 teaspoon ground cinnamon
- 1/4 teaspoon ground nutmeg
- 2 tablespoons unsalted butter, melted

For the Glaze (optional):

- 1 cup (120g) powdered sugar
- 2-3 tablespoons milk

Instructions:

1. **Prepare the Cake:**
    - Preheat your oven to 350°F (175°C). Grease and flour a 9-inch (23cm) round cake pan or line it with parchment paper.
    - In a medium bowl, whisk together the flour, baking powder, baking soda, and salt.
    - In a large bowl, cream together the softened butter and granulated sugar until light and fluffy.
    - Beat in the eggs one at a time, mixing well after each addition.
    - Stir in the sour cream (or yogurt), milk, and vanilla extract until combined.
    - Gradually add the dry ingredients to the wet mixture, mixing until just combined.
    - Gently fold in the chopped peaches.
    - Pour the batter into the prepared cake pan and smooth the top with a spatula.
2. **Prepare the Topping:**

- In a small bowl, combine the granulated sugar, flour, ground cinnamon, and ground nutmeg.
- Sprinkle the topping mixture evenly over the batter.
- Drizzle the melted butter over the top.
3. **Bake the Cake:**
    - Bake in the preheated oven for 35-40 minutes, or until a toothpick inserted into the center comes out clean and the top is golden brown.
    - Allow the cake to cool in the pan for 10 minutes, then transfer to a wire rack to cool completely.
4. **Prepare the Glaze (optional):**
    - In a small bowl, whisk together the powdered sugar and milk until smooth. Adjust the consistency with more milk or powdered sugar if needed.
    - Drizzle the glaze over the cooled cake.
5. **Serve:**
    - Slice and serve the cake at room temperature. It's delicious on its own or with a scoop of vanilla ice cream or a dollop of whipped cream.

Tips:

- **Peaches:** Use fresh peaches for the best flavor, but frozen peaches can be used if fresh ones are not available. Be sure to thaw and drain frozen peaches before adding them to the batter.
- **Topping:** The topping gives the cake a sweet, cobbler-like finish. For extra crunch, you can add a bit of chopped nuts to the topping mixture.
- **Storage:** The cake can be stored in an airtight container at room temperature for up to 3 days or refrigerated for up to a week. It can also be frozen for up to 2 months; thaw in the refrigerator before serving.

Peach Cobbler Cake is a delightful dessert that combines the best of both worlds: the comfort of a cobbler and the lightness of a cake. Enjoy this treat with family and friends for a delicious and satisfying dessert!

Cherry Blossom Cake

Ingredients:

For the Cake:

- 1 1/2 cups (190g) all-purpose flour
- 1 1/2 teaspoons baking powder
- 1/2 teaspoon baking soda
- 1/4 teaspoon salt
- 1/2 cup (115g) unsalted butter, softened
- 1 cup (200g) granulated sugar
- 2 large eggs
- 1/2 cup (120ml) sour cream or plain yogurt
- 1/2 cup (120ml) milk
- 1 teaspoon vanilla extract
- 1 teaspoon almond extract (optional for added depth)
- 1/4 cup (60ml) cherry juice or light cherry syrup (for flavoring)

For the Cherry Blossom Buttercream Frosting:

- 1 cup (230g) unsalted butter, softened
- 4 cups (500g) powdered sugar, sifted
- 2-3 tablespoons milk or cream
- 1 teaspoon vanilla extract
- 1-2 tablespoons cherry juice or light cherry syrup (for flavor and color)
- A few drops of pink or red food coloring (optional, for a hint of color)

For Garnish (optional):

- Edible cherry blossoms or dried cherry blossoms (ensure they are food-grade)
- Fresh cherries

Instructions:

1. **Prepare the Cake:**
    - Preheat your oven to 350°F (175°C). Grease and flour an 8-inch (20cm) round cake pan or line it with parchment paper. You can also use two 8-inch round pans if you prefer a layered cake.
    - In a medium bowl, whisk together the flour, baking powder, baking soda, and salt.
    - In a large bowl, cream together the softened butter and granulated sugar until light and fluffy.
    - Beat in the eggs one at a time, mixing well after each addition.
    - Stir in the sour cream (or yogurt), milk, vanilla extract, almond extract (if using), and cherry juice or syrup until combined.
    - Gradually add the dry ingredients to the wet mixture, mixing until just combined.

- Pour the batter into the prepared cake pan(s) and smooth the top with a spatula.
2. **Bake the Cake:**
    - Bake in the preheated oven for 30-35 minutes, or until a toothpick inserted into the center comes out clean and the cake is golden brown.
    - Allow the cake to cool in the pan for 10 minutes, then transfer to a wire rack to cool completely.
3. **Prepare the Cherry Blossom Buttercream Frosting:**
    - In a large bowl, beat the softened butter until creamy and smooth.
    - Gradually add the powdered sugar, beating well after each addition, until the frosting is smooth and fluffy.
    - Mix in the milk or cream, vanilla extract, and cherry juice or syrup until fully incorporated. Adjust the consistency with more milk or powdered sugar if needed.
    - If desired, add a few drops of pink or red food coloring to achieve a soft, pink hue.
4. **Assemble and Frost the Cake:**
    - Once the cake is completely cooled, spread a layer of frosting on top of one cake layer (if using two layers). Place the second layer on top and frost the top and sides of the cake.
    - Smooth the frosting with a spatula or pipe decorative borders and flowers if desired.
5. **Garnish and Serve:**
    - Garnish with edible cherry blossoms or fresh cherries if desired.
    - Slice and serve the cake at room temperature.

Tips:

- **Cherry Juice:** Cherry juice or syrup can be purchased or made from fresh cherries. If using syrup, make sure it is light and not too thick.
- **Food Coloring:** A small amount of food coloring can be used to achieve a subtle pink color in the frosting. Add gradually to avoid over-coloring.
- **Storage:** The cake can be stored in an airtight container at room temperature for up to 3 days or refrigerated for up to a week. It can also be frozen for up to 2 months; thaw in the refrigerator before serving.

Cherry Blossom Cake is a lovely, elegant dessert that brings the delicate beauty and flavor of cherry blossoms to life. Enjoy this cake as a centerpiece for special occasions or as a charming treat!

Molasses Spice Cake

Ingredients:

For the Cake:

- 1 1/2 cups (190g) all-purpose flour
- 1 1/2 teaspoons baking powder
- 1/2 teaspoon baking soda
- 1/2 teaspoon salt
- 1 tablespoon ground cinnamon
- 1/2 teaspoon ground ginger
- 1/2 teaspoon ground cloves
- 1/2 teaspoon ground nutmeg
- 1/2 cup (115g) unsalted butter, softened
- 1 cup (200g) granulated sugar
- 1/2 cup (120ml) molasses (unsulfured)
- 2 large eggs
- 1/2 cup (120ml) buttermilk or milk
- 1 teaspoon vanilla extract

For the Cream Cheese Frosting (optional):

- 1/2 cup (115g) unsalted butter, softened
- 8 oz (225g) cream cheese, softened
- 3-4 cups (375-500g) powdered sugar, sifted
- 1 teaspoon vanilla extract

For Garnish (optional):

- Ground cinnamon
- Chopped nuts or crystallized ginger

Instructions:

1. **Prepare the Cake:**
    - Preheat your oven to 350°F (175°C). Grease and flour an 8-inch (20cm) round cake pan or line it with parchment paper. You can also use two 8-inch round pans if you prefer a layered cake.
    - In a medium bowl, whisk together the flour, baking powder, baking soda, salt, cinnamon, ginger, cloves, and nutmeg.
    - In a large bowl, cream together the softened butter and granulated sugar until light and fluffy.
    - Beat in the eggs one at a time, mixing well after each addition.
    - Stir in the molasses until fully incorporated.
    - Gradually add the dry ingredients to the wet mixture, alternating with the buttermilk (or milk), beginning and ending with the flour mixture. Mix until just combined.

- Stir in the vanilla extract.
- Pour the batter into the prepared cake pan and smooth the top with a spatula.

2. **Bake the Cake:**
   - Bake in the preheated oven for 30-35 minutes, or until a toothpick inserted into the center comes out clean and the cake is set.
   - Allow the cake to cool in the pan for 10 minutes, then transfer to a wire rack to cool completely.
3. **Prepare the Cream Cheese Frosting (optional):**
   - In a large bowl, beat the softened butter and cream cheese until creamy and smooth.
   - Gradually add the powdered sugar, beating well after each addition, until the frosting is smooth and fluffy.
   - Mix in the vanilla extract.
4. **Frost and Garnish:**
   - Once the cake is completely cooled, spread the cream cheese frosting evenly over the top and sides of the cake if using.
   - Garnish with a sprinkle of ground cinnamon or chopped nuts/crystallized ginger if desired.
5. **Serve:**
   - Slice and serve the cake at room temperature. It pairs wonderfully with a cup of tea or coffee.

Tips:

- **Molasses:** Use unsulfured molasses for the best flavor. Sulfured molasses has a more bitter taste.
- **Spices:** Adjust the spice amounts to suit your taste. If you like it spicier, you can add a bit more cinnamon or ginger.
- **Storage:** The cake can be stored in an airtight container at room temperature for up to 3 days or refrigerated for up to a week. It can also be frozen for up to 2 months; thaw in the refrigerator before serving.

Molasses Spice Cake is a wonderfully flavorful dessert that brings warmth and comfort with every bite. Enjoy the rich taste of molasses combined with aromatic spices in this delicious cake!

Rhubarb Almond Cake

Ingredients:

For the Cake:

- 1 1/2 cups (190g) all-purpose flour
- 1/2 cup (50g) almond flour
- 1 1/2 teaspoons baking powder
- 1/2 teaspoon baking soda
- 1/4 teaspoon salt
- 1/2 cup (115g) unsalted butter, softened
- 1 cup (200g) granulated sugar
- 2 large eggs
- 1 teaspoon vanilla extract
- 1/2 cup (120ml) buttermilk or milk
- 1 cup (150g) chopped rhubarb (fresh or frozen, thawed and drained)

For the Almond Streusel Topping:

- 1/4 cup (30g) all-purpose flour
- 1/4 cup (30g) almond flour
- 1/4 cup (50g) granulated sugar
- 1/4 cup (60g) unsalted butter, cold and cut into small pieces
- 1/4 cup (25g) sliced almonds

For the Glaze (optional):

- 1/2 cup (60g) powdered sugar
- 1-2 tablespoons milk

Instructions:

1. **Prepare the Cake:**
   - Preheat your oven to 350°F (175°C). Grease and flour a 9-inch (23cm) round cake pan or line it with parchment paper.
   - In a medium bowl, whisk together the all-purpose flour, almond flour, baking powder, baking soda, and salt.
   - In a large bowl, cream together the softened butter and granulated sugar until light and fluffy.
   - Beat in the eggs one at a time, mixing well after each addition.
   - Stir in the vanilla extract.
   - Gradually add the dry ingredients to the wet mixture, alternating with the buttermilk (or milk), beginning and ending with the flour mixture. Mix until just combined.
   - Gently fold in the chopped rhubarb.
   - Pour the batter into the prepared cake pan and smooth the top with a spatula.
2. **Prepare the Almond Streusel Topping:**

- In a small bowl, combine the all-purpose flour, almond flour, and granulated sugar.
       - Cut in the cold butter using a pastry cutter or your fingers until the mixture resembles coarse crumbs.
       - Stir in the sliced almonds.
       - Sprinkle the streusel topping evenly over the batter in the cake pan.
  3. **Bake the Cake:**
       - Bake in the preheated oven for 35-40 minutes, or until a toothpick inserted into the center comes out clean and the top is golden brown.
       - Allow the cake to cool in the pan for 10 minutes, then transfer to a wire rack to cool completely.
  4. **Prepare the Glaze (optional):**
       - In a small bowl, whisk together the powdered sugar and milk until smooth. Adjust the consistency with more milk or powdered sugar if needed.
       - Drizzle the glaze over the cooled cake.
  5. **Serve:**
       - Slice and serve the cake at room temperature. It's delicious on its own or with a dollop of whipped cream or a scoop of vanilla ice cream.

Tips:

- **Rhubarb:** If using frozen rhubarb, make sure it is thawed and well-drained to prevent excess moisture in the cake. Fresh rhubarb works perfectly as well.
- **Almond Flour:** Almond flour adds a nutty flavor and moist texture to the cake. You can also use almond meal if that's what you have on hand.
- **Storage:** The cake can be stored in an airtight container at room temperature for up to 3 days or in the refrigerator for up to a week. It can also be frozen for up to 2 months; thaw in the refrigerator before serving.

Rhubarb Almond Cake is a delightful combination of flavors and textures, offering a sweet and slightly tart profile with a crunchy almond topping. Enjoy this cake as a special treat or dessert for any occasion!

Hummingbird Cake

Ingredients:

For the Cake:

- 1 1/2 cups (190g) all-purpose flour
- 1 1/2 teaspoons baking powder
- 1/2 teaspoon baking soda
- 1/4 teaspoon salt
- 1 teaspoon ground cinnamon
- 1/2 teaspoon ground nutmeg
- 1/2 cup (115g) unsalted butter, softened
- 1 cup (200g) granulated sugar
- 1/2 cup (100g) packed light brown sugar
- 2 large eggs
- 1 cup (240ml) crushed pineapple, drained
- 1 cup (240ml) mashed ripe banana (about 2 bananas)
- 1/2 cup (120ml) chopped pecans or walnuts (optional)
- 1 teaspoon vanilla extract

For the Cream Cheese Frosting:

- 1/2 cup (115g) unsalted butter, softened
- 8 oz (225g) cream cheese, softened
- 4 cups (500g) powdered sugar, sifted
- 1 teaspoon vanilla extract

For Garnish (optional):

- Additional chopped pecans or walnuts
- A sprinkle of cinnamon

Instructions:

1. **Prepare the Cake:**
    - Preheat your oven to 350°F (175°C). Grease and flour two 9-inch (23cm) round cake pans or line them with parchment paper.
    - In a medium bowl, whisk together the flour, baking powder, baking soda, salt, cinnamon, and nutmeg.
    - In a large bowl, cream together the softened butter, granulated sugar, and brown sugar until light and fluffy.
    - Beat in the eggs one at a time, mixing well after each addition.
    - Stir in the vanilla extract.
    - Gradually add the dry ingredients to the wet mixture, mixing until just combined.
    - Gently fold in the crushed pineapple, mashed banana, and chopped pecans or walnuts (if using).
    - Divide the batter evenly between the prepared cake pans and smooth the tops with a spatula.

2. **Bake the Cake:**
   - Bake in the preheated oven for 25-30 minutes, or until a toothpick inserted into the center comes out clean and the cakes are golden brown.
   - Allow the cakes to cool in the pans for 10 minutes, then transfer to a wire rack to cool completely.
3. **Prepare the Cream Cheese Frosting:**
   - In a large bowl, beat the softened butter and cream cheese until creamy and smooth.
   - Gradually add the powdered sugar, beating well after each addition, until the frosting is smooth and fluffy.
   - Mix in the vanilla extract.
4. **Assemble and Frost the Cake:**
   - Once the cakes are completely cooled, place one layer on a serving plate or cake stand.
   - Spread a layer of cream cheese frosting over the top.
   - Place the second cake layer on top and frost the top and sides of the cake with the remaining cream cheese frosting.
   - Garnish with additional chopped pecans or walnuts and a sprinkle of cinnamon if desired.
5. **Serve:**
   - Slice and serve the cake at room temperature. It pairs beautifully with a cup of coffee or tea.

Tips:

- **Ripeness of Bananas:** Use very ripe bananas for the best flavor and sweetness.
- **Pineapple:** Ensure the crushed pineapple is well-drained to avoid excess moisture in the cake.
- **Storage:** The cake can be stored in an airtight container in the refrigerator for up to a week. It can also be frozen for up to 2 months; thaw in the refrigerator before serving.

Hummingbird Cake is a moist and flavorful cake that's sure to impress your family and friends with its rich combination of flavors. Enjoy this Southern classic as a special treat for any occasion!

Maple Bacon Cake

Ingredients:

For the Cake:

- 2 cups (250g) all-purpose flour
- 1 1/2 teaspoons baking powder
- 1/2 teaspoon baking soda
- 1/2 teaspoon salt
- 1 teaspoon ground cinnamon
- 1/2 cup (115g) unsalted butter, softened
- 1 cup (200g) granulated sugar
- 1/2 cup (100g) packed light brown sugar
- 2 large eggs
- 1 cup (240ml) buttermilk or milk
- 1/2 cup (120ml) pure maple syrup
- 1 teaspoon vanilla extract
- 1/2 cup (75g) finely chopped cooked bacon (about 4-5 slices)

For the Maple Cream Cheese Frosting:

- 1/2 cup (115g) unsalted butter, softened
- 8 oz (225g) cream cheese, softened
- 3-4 cups (375-500g) powdered sugar, sifted
- 1/4 cup (60ml) pure maple syrup
- 1 teaspoon vanilla extract
- A pinch of salt (optional)

For Garnish (optional):

- Additional crumbled bacon
- Maple syrup drizzle

Instructions:

1. **Prepare the Cake:**
    - Preheat your oven to 350°F (175°C). Grease and flour two 9-inch (23cm) round cake pans or line them with parchment paper.
    - In a medium bowl, whisk together the flour, baking powder, baking soda, salt, and cinnamon.
    - In a large bowl, cream together the softened butter, granulated sugar, and brown sugar until light and fluffy.
    - Beat in the eggs one at a time, mixing well after each addition.
    - Stir in the maple syrup and vanilla extract.
    - Gradually add the dry ingredients to the wet mixture, alternating with the buttermilk (or milk), beginning and ending with the flour mixture. Mix until just combined.
    - Gently fold in the finely chopped bacon.

- Divide the batter evenly between the prepared cake pans and smooth the tops with a spatula.
2. **Bake the Cake:**
    - Bake in the preheated oven for 25-30 minutes, or until a toothpick inserted into the center comes out clean and the cakes are golden brown.
    - Allow the cakes to cool in the pans for 10 minutes, then transfer to a wire rack to cool completely.
3. **Prepare the Maple Cream Cheese Frosting:**
    - In a large bowl, beat the softened butter and cream cheese until creamy and smooth.
    - Gradually add the powdered sugar, beating well after each addition, until the frosting is smooth and fluffy.
    - Mix in the maple syrup and vanilla extract. Adjust with a pinch of salt if desired for balance.
4. **Assemble and Frost the Cake:**
    - Once the cakes are completely cooled, place one layer on a serving plate or cake stand.
    - Spread a layer of maple cream cheese frosting over the top.
    - Place the second cake layer on top and frost the top and sides of the cake with the remaining frosting.
    - Garnish with additional crumbled bacon and a drizzle of maple syrup if desired.
5. **Serve:**
    - Slice and serve the cake at room temperature. It pairs beautifully with a cup of coffee or tea.

Tips:

- **Bacon:** For best results, use thick-cut bacon and cook it until crispy. Drain on paper towels and chop finely before adding to the batter.
- **Maple Syrup:** Use pure maple syrup for the best flavor. Avoid imitation maple syrup.
- **Storage:** The cake can be stored in an airtight container at room temperature for up to 3 days or refrigerated for up to a week. It can also be frozen for up to 2 months; thaw in the refrigerator before serving.

Maple Bacon Cake is a decadent treat that combines the sweetness of maple syrup with the savory crunch of bacon. It's perfect for brunches, special occasions, or anytime you want a unique and flavorful dessert!

Red Velvet Cake

Ingredients:

For the Cake:

- 2 1/2 cups (315g) all-purpose flour
- 1 1/2 cups (300g) granulated sugar
- 1 teaspoon baking powder
- 1 teaspoon baking soda
- 1/2 teaspoon salt
- 1 tablespoon cocoa powder (unsweetened)
- 1 cup (240ml) vegetable oil
- 1 cup (240ml) buttermilk
- 2 large eggs
- 2 tablespoons red food coloring (liquid or gel)
- 1 teaspoon vanilla extract
- 1 teaspoon white vinegar

For the Cream Cheese Frosting:

- 1/2 cup (115g) unsalted butter, softened
- 8 oz (225g) cream cheese, softened
- 4 cups (500g) powdered sugar, sifted
- 1 teaspoon vanilla extract

For Garnish (optional):

- Red velvet cake crumbs
- Fresh berries or edible flowers

Instructions:

1. **Prepare the Cake:**
    - Preheat your oven to 350°F (175°C). Grease and flour two 9-inch (23cm) round cake pans or line them with parchment paper.
    - In a medium bowl, whisk together the flour, granulated sugar, baking powder, baking soda, salt, and cocoa powder.
    - In a large bowl, combine the vegetable oil, buttermilk, eggs, red food coloring, vanilla extract, and white vinegar. Mix well.
    - Gradually add the dry ingredients to the wet ingredients, mixing until just combined and smooth.
    - Divide the batter evenly between the prepared cake pans and smooth the tops with a spatula.
2. **Bake the Cake:**
    - Bake in the preheated oven for 25-30 minutes, or until a toothpick inserted into the center comes out clean and the cakes are set.
    - Allow the cakes to cool in the pans for 10 minutes, then transfer them to a wire rack to cool completely.

3. **Prepare the Cream Cheese Frosting:**
   - In a large bowl, beat the softened butter and cream cheese until creamy and smooth.
   - Gradually add the powdered sugar, beating well after each addition until the frosting is light and fluffy.
   - Mix in the vanilla extract.
4. **Assemble and Frost the Cake:**
   - Once the cakes are completely cooled, place one layer on a serving plate or cake stand.
   - Spread a layer of cream cheese frosting over the top.
   - Place the second cake layer on top and frost the top and sides of the cake with the remaining cream cheese frosting.
   - Garnish with red velvet cake crumbs, fresh berries, or edible flowers if desired.
5. **Serve:**
   - Slice and serve the cake at room temperature. It pairs wonderfully with a cup of coffee or tea.

Tips:

- **Red Food Coloring:** Gel food coloring is recommended for a more vibrant color without affecting the cake's texture. If using liquid food coloring, you may need to use more.
- **Buttermilk:** If you don't have buttermilk, you can make a substitute by adding 1 tablespoon of white vinegar or lemon juice to 1 cup of milk. Let it sit for 5 minutes before using.
- **Storage:** The cake can be stored in an airtight container at room temperature for up to 3 days or in the refrigerator for up to a week. It can also be frozen for up to 2 months; thaw in the refrigerator before serving.

Red Velvet Cake is a showstopper dessert with its striking color and rich flavor. Enjoy this classic treat for birthdays, holidays, or any special occasion!

Prairie Berry Cake

Ingredients:

For the Cake:

- 1 1/2 cups (190g) all-purpose flour
- 1 1/2 teaspoons baking powder
- 1/2 teaspoon baking soda
- 1/4 teaspoon salt
- 1/2 cup (115g) unsalted butter, softened
- 1 cup (200g) granulated sugar
- 2 large eggs
- 1 teaspoon vanilla extract
- 1/2 cup (120ml) buttermilk or milk
- 1 cup (150g) mixed berries (fresh or frozen, such as Saskatoon berries, raspberries, or blueberries)

For the Berry Swirl:

- 1/2 cup (75g) mixed berries (fresh or frozen)
- 1/4 cup (50g) granulated sugar
- 1 tablespoon lemon juice

For the Glaze (optional):

- 1/2 cup (60g) powdered sugar
- 1-2 tablespoons milk

For Garnish (optional):

- Fresh berries
- Mint leaves

Instructions:

1. **Prepare the Berry Swirl:**
    - In a small saucepan, combine 1/2 cup of mixed berries, granulated sugar, and lemon juice.
    - Cook over medium heat, stirring occasionally, until the berries break down and the mixture thickens slightly, about 5-7 minutes.
    - Remove from heat and let cool.
2. **Prepare the Cake:**
    - Preheat your oven to 350°F (175°C). Grease and flour a 9-inch (23cm) round cake pan or line it with parchment paper.
    - In a medium bowl, whisk together the flour, baking powder, baking soda, and salt.
    - In a large bowl, cream together the softened butter and granulated sugar until light and fluffy.
    - Beat in the eggs one at a time, mixing well after each addition.
    - Stir in the vanilla extract.

- Gradually add the dry ingredients to the wet mixture, alternating with the buttermilk (or milk), beginning and ending with the flour mixture. Mix until just combined.
- Gently fold in the 1 cup of mixed berries.

3. **Assemble the Cake:**
   - Pour half of the cake batter into the prepared cake pan.
   - Drop spoonfuls of the berry swirl mixture over the batter and use a knife or skewer to gently swirl it into the batter.
   - Pour the remaining batter on top and smooth the surface.
   - Drop spoonfuls of the remaining berry swirl over the top and swirl again.
4. **Bake the Cake:**
   - Bake in the preheated oven for 30-35 minutes, or until a toothpick inserted into the center comes out clean and the cake is golden brown.
   - Allow the cake to cool in the pan for 10 minutes, then transfer to a wire rack to cool completely.
5. **Prepare the Glaze (optional):**
   - In a small bowl, whisk together the powdered sugar and milk until smooth. Adjust the consistency with more milk or powdered sugar if needed.
   - Drizzle the glaze over the cooled cake.
6. **Serve:**
   - Garnish with fresh berries and mint leaves if desired.
   - Slice and serve the cake at room temperature.

Tips:

- **Berry Variations:** Feel free to use any combination of berries you prefer. Fresh berries are best, but frozen berries can also be used if thawed and drained well.
- **Buttermilk Substitute:** If you don't have buttermilk, you can use milk with a splash of lemon juice or vinegar.
- **Storage:** The cake can be stored in an airtight container at room temperature for up to 3 days or refrigerated for up to a week. It can also be frozen for up to 2 months; thaw in the refrigerator before serving.

Prairie Berry Cake is a flavorful dessert that highlights the natural sweetness and tartness of prairie berries, making it a wonderful treat for any occasion. Enjoy!

Victoria Sponge Cake

Ingredients:

For the Cake:

- 1 cup (225g) unsalted butter, softened
- 1 cup (225g) granulated sugar
- 2 large eggs
- 1 1/2 cups (190g) all-purpose flour
- 1 1/2 teaspoons baking powder
- 1/4 teaspoon salt
- 1/4 cup (60ml) whole milk
- 1 teaspoon vanilla extract

For the Filling:

- 1/2 cup (160g) raspberry or strawberry jam (or your preferred fruit jam)
- 1/2 cup (120ml) heavy cream

For the Dusting:

- Powdered sugar

Instructions:

1. **Prepare the Cake:**
   - Preheat your oven to 350°F (175°C). Grease and flour two 8-inch (20cm) round cake pans or line them with parchment paper.
   - In a medium bowl, sift together the flour, baking powder, and salt. Set aside.
   - In a large bowl, cream together the softened butter and granulated sugar until light and fluffy.
   - Beat in the eggs one at a time, mixing well after each addition.
   - Stir in the vanilla extract.
   - Gradually add the dry ingredients to the wet mixture, alternating with the milk. Mix until just combined and smooth.
   - Divide the batter evenly between the prepared cake pans and smooth the tops with a spatula.
2. **Bake the Cake:**
   - Bake in the preheated oven for 20-25 minutes, or until a toothpick inserted into the center comes out clean and the cakes are golden brown.
   - Allow the cakes to cool in the pans for 10 minutes, then transfer to a wire rack to cool completely.
3. **Prepare the Filling:**
   - Whip the heavy cream until stiff peaks form. You can use a hand mixer or a stand mixer fitted with a whisk attachment.
   - Once the cakes are completely cooled, spread the jam over the top of one cake layer.
   - Spread the whipped cream over the jam.

4. **Assemble the Cake:**
    - Place the second cake layer on top of the jam and cream.
    - Dust the top of the cake with powdered sugar.
5. **Serve:**
    - Slice and serve the cake at room temperature. It's perfect for afternoon tea or as a light dessert.

Tips:

- **Cake Layers:** Make sure the cake layers are completely cooled before assembling to prevent the cream from melting.
- **Jam:** Use a good quality fruit jam for the best flavor. You can also use lemon curd or fresh fruit if preferred.
- **Storage:** The cake is best enjoyed fresh but can be stored in an airtight container at room temperature for up to 2 days. Refrigerate if you plan to keep it longer.

Victoria Sponge Cake is celebrated for its simplicity and delightful taste. Enjoy making and serving this classic British cake!

Chocolate Avocado Cake

Ingredients:

For the Cake:

- 1 cup (230g) ripe avocado flesh (about 2 small avocados)
- 1 cup (200g) granulated sugar
- 2 large eggs
- 1 teaspoon vanilla extract
- 1 cup (125g) all-purpose flour
- 1/2 cup (50g) unsweetened cocoa powder
- 1 teaspoon baking powder
- 1/2 teaspoon baking soda
- 1/4 teaspoon salt
- 1/2 cup (120ml) buttermilk or milk
- 1/2 cup (120ml) brewed coffee (optional, enhances the chocolate flavor)

For the Chocolate Frosting:

- 1/2 cup (115g) ripe avocado flesh
- 1/2 cup (115g) unsalted butter, softened
- 1 1/2 cups (190g) powdered sugar
- 1/2 cup (50g) unsweetened cocoa powder
- 1 teaspoon vanilla extract
- A pinch of salt
- 1-2 tablespoons milk or heavy cream (if needed for consistency)

For Garnish (optional):

- Shaved chocolate
- Fresh berries
- Mint leaves

Instructions:

1. **Prepare the Cake:**
    - Preheat your oven to 350°F (175°C). Grease and flour an 8-inch (20cm) round cake pan or line it with parchment paper.
    - In a large bowl, mash the avocado flesh until smooth. You should have about 1 cup of mashed avocado.
    - Add the granulated sugar to the avocado and mix well.
    - Beat in the eggs one at a time, then stir in the vanilla extract.
    - In a separate bowl, whisk together the flour, cocoa powder, baking powder, baking soda, and salt.
    - Gradually add the dry ingredients to the wet ingredients, alternating with the buttermilk (or milk) and coffee (if using). Mix until just combined and smooth.
    - Pour the batter into the prepared cake pan and smooth the top with a spatula.

2. **Bake the Cake:**
   - Bake in the preheated oven for 25-30 minutes, or until a toothpick inserted into the center comes out clean and the cake is set.
   - Allow the cake to cool in the pan for 10 minutes, then transfer to a wire rack to cool completely.
3. **Prepare the Chocolate Frosting:**
   - In a medium bowl, beat the mashed avocado and softened butter until creamy and smooth.
   - Gradually add the powdered sugar and cocoa powder, beating well after each addition.
   - Mix in the vanilla extract and a pinch of salt.
   - If needed, adjust the consistency with milk or heavy cream, adding a little at a time until the frosting is smooth and spreadable.
4. **Assemble the Cake:**
   - Once the cake is completely cooled, spread the chocolate frosting over the top and sides of the cake.
   - Garnish with shaved chocolate, fresh berries, or mint leaves if desired.
5. **Serve:**
   - Slice and serve the cake at room temperature. It pairs beautifully with a glass of cold milk or a cup of coffee.

Tips:

- **Avocado:** Ensure the avocados are fully ripe for the best texture and flavor.
- **Coffee:** The brewed coffee enhances the chocolate flavor but can be omitted if preferred.
- **Storage:** The cake can be stored in an airtight container at room temperature for up to 3 days or refrigerated for up to a week. The frosting may need to be slightly re-whipped if refrigerated.

Chocolate Avocado Cake is a deliciously moist and healthier alternative to traditional chocolate cake, offering a unique and satisfying treat. Enjoy!

Blueberry Lemon Buttermilk Cake

Ingredients:

For the Cake:

- 1 1/2 cups (190g) all-purpose flour
- 1 1/2 teaspoons baking powder
- 1/2 teaspoon baking soda
- 1/4 teaspoon salt
- 1/2 cup (115g) unsalted butter, softened
- 1 cup (200g) granulated sugar
- 2 large eggs
- 1 tablespoon lemon zest (about 1 lemon)
- 2 tablespoons fresh lemon juice
- 1 cup (240ml) buttermilk
- 1 1/2 cups (225g) fresh blueberries (or frozen, if fresh are unavailable)

For the Lemon Glaze (optional):

- 1 cup (120g) powdered sugar
- 2-3 tablespoons fresh lemon juice

For Garnish (optional):

- Additional blueberries
- Lemon zest

Instructions:

1. **Prepare the Cake:**
   - Preheat your oven to 350°F (175°C). Grease and flour a 9-inch (23cm) round cake pan or line it with parchment paper.
   - In a medium bowl, whisk together the flour, baking powder, baking soda, and salt. Set aside.
   - In a large bowl, cream together the softened butter and granulated sugar until light and fluffy.
   - Beat in the eggs one at a time, mixing well after each addition.
   - Stir in the lemon zest and lemon juice.
   - Gradually add the dry ingredients to the wet mixture, alternating with the buttermilk. Begin and end with the flour mixture. Mix until just combined and smooth.
   - Gently fold in the blueberries.
2. **Bake the Cake:**
   - Pour the batter into the prepared cake pan and smooth the top with a spatula.
   - Bake in the preheated oven for 30-35 minutes, or until a toothpick inserted into the center comes out clean and the cake is golden brown.
   - Allow the cake to cool in the pan for 10 minutes, then transfer to a wire rack to cool completely.

3. **Prepare the Lemon Glaze (optional):**
   - In a small bowl, whisk together the powdered sugar and lemon juice until smooth. Adjust the consistency with more lemon juice or powdered sugar as needed.
4. **Assemble and Garnish:**
   - Once the cake is completely cooled, drizzle the lemon glaze over the top, allowing it to drip down the sides.
   - Garnish with additional blueberries and lemon zest if desired.
5. **Serve:**
   - Slice and serve the cake at room temperature. It pairs beautifully with a cup of tea or coffee.

Tips:

- **Blueberries:** If using frozen blueberries, do not thaw them before adding to the batter. Toss them in a little flour before folding into the batter to prevent them from sinking.
- **Buttermilk Substitute:** If you don't have buttermilk, you can use milk with a tablespoon of lemon juice or vinegar added.
- **Storage:** The cake can be stored in an airtight container at room temperature for up to 3 days or refrigerated for up to a week. It can also be frozen for up to 2 months; thaw in the refrigerator before serving.

Blueberry Lemon Buttermilk Cake is a vibrant and flavorful cake that's perfect for a variety of occasions. Enjoy this delightful treat!

Apple Cinnamon Cake

Ingredients:

For the Cake:

- 1 1/2 cups (190g) all-purpose flour
- 1 1/2 teaspoons baking powder
- 1/2 teaspoon baking soda
- 1/2 teaspoon salt
- 1 teaspoon ground cinnamon
- 1/2 teaspoon ground nutmeg (optional)
- 1/2 cup (115g) unsalted butter, softened
- 1 cup (200g) granulated sugar
- 2 large eggs
- 1 teaspoon vanilla extract
- 1 cup (240ml) buttermilk or milk
- 2 cups (about 2 medium) peeled and diced apples (e.g., Granny Smith or Honeycrisp)
- 1/4 cup (30g) packed light brown sugar (for topping)
- 1 tablespoon ground cinnamon (for topping)

For the Optional Glaze:

- 1 cup (120g) powdered sugar
- 1-2 tablespoons milk
- 1/2 teaspoon vanilla extract

Instructions:

1. **Prepare the Cake:**
    - Preheat your oven to 350°F (175°C). Grease and flour a 9-inch (23cm) round cake pan or line it with parchment paper.
    - In a medium bowl, whisk together the flour, baking powder, baking soda, salt, cinnamon, and nutmeg (if using). Set aside.
    - In a large bowl, cream together the softened butter and granulated sugar until light and fluffy.
    - Beat in the eggs one at a time, mixing well after each addition.
    - Stir in the vanilla extract.
    - Gradually add the dry ingredients to the wet mixture, alternating with the buttermilk (or milk). Begin and end with the flour mixture. Mix until just combined and smooth.
    - Fold in the diced apples.
2. **Add Topping:**
    - In a small bowl, mix together the brown sugar and cinnamon.
    - Sprinkle this mixture evenly over the top of the batter in the cake pan.
3. **Bake the Cake:**
    - Bake in the preheated oven for 35-40 minutes, or until a toothpick inserted into the center comes out clean and the cake is golden brown.

- Allow the cake to cool in the pan for 10 minutes, then transfer to a wire rack to cool completely.
4. **Prepare the Glaze (optional):**
    - In a small bowl, whisk together the powdered sugar, milk, and vanilla extract until smooth. Adjust the consistency with more milk or powdered sugar if needed.
    - Drizzle the glaze over the cooled cake.
5. **Serve:**
    - Slice and serve the cake at room temperature. It's perfect on its own or with a cup of coffee or tea.

Tips:

- **Apples:** Use firm, tart apples that hold their shape during baking, like Granny Smith or Honeycrisp.
- **Buttermilk Substitute:** If you don't have buttermilk, you can use milk with a tablespoon of lemon juice or vinegar added.
- **Storage:** The cake can be stored in an airtight container at room temperature for up to 3 days or refrigerated for up to a week. It can also be frozen for up to 2 months; thaw in the refrigerator before serving.

Apple Cinnamon Cake is a delightful treat with a warm, comforting flavor that's sure to please. Enjoy this classic dessert!

Maple Cream Cheese Cake

Ingredients:

For the Cake:

- 1 1/2 cups (190g) all-purpose flour
- 1 1/2 teaspoons baking powder
- 1/2 teaspoon baking soda
- 1/4 teaspoon salt
- 1 teaspoon ground cinnamon
- 1/4 teaspoon ground nutmeg (optional)
- 1/2 cup (115g) unsalted butter, softened
- 1 cup (200g) granulated sugar
- 1/2 cup (120ml) pure maple syrup
- 2 large eggs
- 1 teaspoon vanilla extract
- 1/2 cup (120ml) buttermilk or milk
- 4 oz (115g) cream cheese, softened

For the Cream Cheese Frosting:

- 8 oz (225g) cream cheese, softened
- 1/2 cup (115g) unsalted butter, softened
- 4 cups (500g) powdered sugar
- 1/4 cup (60ml) pure maple syrup
- 1 teaspoon vanilla extract

For Garnish (optional):

- Chopped pecans or walnuts
- Extra maple syrup for drizzling

Instructions:

1. **Prepare the Cake:**
    - Preheat your oven to 350°F (175°C). Grease and flour a 9-inch (23cm) round cake pan or line it with parchment paper.
    - In a medium bowl, whisk together the flour, baking powder, baking soda, salt, cinnamon, and nutmeg (if using). Set aside.
    - In a large bowl, cream together the softened butter and granulated sugar until light and fluffy.
    - Beat in the maple syrup until well combined.
    - Add the eggs one at a time, mixing well after each addition.
    - Stir in the vanilla extract.
    - Gradually add the dry ingredients to the wet mixture, alternating with the buttermilk (or milk). Begin and end with the flour mixture. Mix until just combined and smooth.
    - Fold in the 4 oz of cream cheese until evenly distributed in the batter.

- Pour the batter into the prepared cake pan and smooth the top with a spatula.
2. **Bake the Cake:**
    - Bake in the preheated oven for 30-35 minutes, or until a toothpick inserted into the center comes out clean and the cake is golden brown.
    - Allow the cake to cool in the pan for 10 minutes, then transfer to a wire rack to cool completely.
3. **Prepare the Cream Cheese Frosting:**
    - In a large bowl, beat the softened cream cheese and butter until creamy and smooth.
    - Gradually add the powdered sugar, beating well after each addition.
    - Mix in the maple syrup and vanilla extract until well combined and smooth.
4. **Assemble the Cake:**
    - Once the cake is completely cooled, spread the cream cheese frosting over the top and sides of the cake.
    - Garnish with chopped pecans or walnuts and a drizzle of maple syrup if desired.
5. **Serve:**
    - Slice and serve the cake at room temperature. It pairs beautifully with a cup of coffee or tea.

Tips:

- **Maple Syrup:** Use pure maple syrup for the best flavor. Avoid imitation syrup or pancake syrup.
- **Cream Cheese:** Ensure the cream cheese is well softened before mixing to avoid lumps in the frosting.
- **Storage:** The cake can be stored in an airtight container at room temperature for up to 3 days or refrigerated for up to a week. It can also be frozen for up to 2 months; thaw in the refrigerator before serving.

Maple Cream Cheese Cake is a delectable treat that combines the rich flavors of maple and cream cheese into a moist and indulgent cake. Enjoy this delightful dessert!

Almond Joy Cake

Ingredients:

For the Chocolate Cake:

- 1 3/4 cups (220g) all-purpose flour
- 1 1/2 teaspoons baking powder
- 1/2 teaspoon baking soda
- 1/4 teaspoon salt
- 1/2 cup (115g) unsalted butter, softened
- 1 cup (200g) granulated sugar
- 1/2 cup (100g) packed brown sugar
- 2 large eggs
- 1 teaspoon vanilla extract
- 1 cup (240ml) buttermilk or milk
- 1/2 cup (50g) unsweetened cocoa powder
- 1/2 cup (120ml) boiling water

For the Coconut Filling:

- 1 1/2 cups (150g) sweetened shredded coconut
- 1/2 cup (120ml) sweetened condensed milk
- 1/2 cup (115g) unsalted butter, softened

For the Chocolate Ganache:

- 1 cup (175g) semisweet chocolate chips
- 1/2 cup (120ml) heavy cream

For Garnish:

- 1/2 cup (75g) whole almonds (toasted if preferred)
- Additional shredded coconut (optional)

Instructions:

1. **Prepare the Chocolate Cake:**
    - Preheat your oven to 350°F (175°C). Grease and flour two 8-inch (20cm) round cake pans or line them with parchment paper.
    - In a medium bowl, whisk together the flour, baking powder, baking soda, and salt. Set aside.
    - In a large bowl, cream together the softened butter, granulated sugar, and brown sugar until light and fluffy.
    - Beat in the eggs one at a time, mixing well after each addition.
    - Stir in the vanilla extract.
    - In a separate bowl, mix the cocoa powder with the boiling water until smooth.
    - Gradually add the dry ingredients to the wet mixture, alternating with the buttermilk (or milk). Mix until just combined.
    - Stir in the cocoa mixture until smooth and fully incorporated.

- Divide the batter evenly between the prepared cake pans and smooth the tops with a spatula.
- Bake for 25-30 minutes, or until a toothpick inserted into the center comes out clean. Allow the cakes to cool in the pans for 10 minutes before transferring to a wire rack to cool completely.

2. **Prepare the Coconut Filling:**
   - In a medium bowl, beat together the shredded coconut, sweetened condensed milk, and softened butter until well combined and creamy.
3. **Prepare the Chocolate Ganache:**
   - In a heatproof bowl, combine the chocolate chips and heavy cream.
   - Microwave in 30-second intervals, stirring after each, until the chocolate is melted and smooth. Let cool slightly before using.
4. **Assemble the Cake:**
   - Place one layer of the chocolate cake on a serving plate or cake stand.
   - Spread the coconut filling evenly over the top of this layer.
   - Place the second layer of cake on top of the coconut filling.
   - Pour the chocolate ganache over the top of the cake, allowing it to drizzle down the sides.
5. **Garnish and Serve:**
   - Garnish the top of the cake with whole almonds and additional shredded coconut if desired.
   - Slice and serve at room temperature. Enjoy with a cup of coffee or tea!

Tips:

- **Toasting Almonds:** To enhance the flavor, you can toast the almonds in a dry skillet over medium heat until golden brown and fragrant.
- **Cake Layers:** Make sure the cakes are completely cooled before assembling to avoid melting the coconut filling.
- **Storage:** The cake can be stored in an airtight container at room temperature for up to 3 days or refrigerated for up to a week. It can also be frozen for up to 2 months; thaw in the refrigerator before serving.

Almond Joy Cake is a rich, indulgent dessert that brings together the classic flavors of chocolate, coconut, and almonds in a delightful cake. Enjoy this treat for any special occasion or as a well-deserved indulgence!

Whiskey and Honey Cake

Ingredients:

For the Cake:

- 1 1/2 cups (190g) all-purpose flour
- 1 1/2 teaspoons baking powder
- 1/2 teaspoon baking soda
- 1/4 teaspoon salt
- 1/2 teaspoon ground cinnamon (optional)
- 1/2 cup (115g) unsalted butter, softened
- 1/2 cup (100g) granulated sugar
- 1/2 cup (120ml) honey
- 2 large eggs
- 1/2 cup (120ml) whiskey (such as bourbon or rye)
- 1 teaspoon vanilla extract
- 1/2 cup (120ml) buttermilk or milk

For the Whiskey Glaze:

- 1 cup (120g) powdered sugar
- 2 tablespoons whiskey
- 1-2 tablespoons milk (if needed for consistency)

For Garnish (optional):

- Toasted pecans or walnuts
- Drizzle of extra honey

Instructions:

1. **Prepare the Cake:**
   - Preheat your oven to 350°F (175°C). Grease and flour an 8-inch (20cm) round cake pan or line it with parchment paper.
   - In a medium bowl, whisk together the flour, baking powder, baking soda, salt, and cinnamon (if using). Set aside.
   - In a large bowl, cream together the softened butter and granulated sugar until light and fluffy.
   - Add the honey and beat until well combined.
   - Beat in the eggs one at a time, mixing well after each addition.
   - Stir in the whiskey and vanilla extract.
   - Gradually add the dry ingredients to the wet mixture, alternating with the buttermilk (or milk). Begin and end with the flour mixture. Mix until just combined and smooth.
   - Pour the batter into the prepared cake pan and smooth the top with a spatula.
2. **Bake the Cake:**
   - Bake in the preheated oven for 30-35 minutes, or until a toothpick inserted into the center comes out clean and the cake is golden brown.

- Allow the cake to cool in the pan for 10 minutes, then transfer to a wire rack to cool completely.
3. **Prepare the Whiskey Glaze:**
    - In a small bowl, whisk together the powdered sugar and whiskey until smooth.
    - If needed, adjust the consistency with milk, adding a little at a time until the glaze is pourable.
4. **Assemble and Garnish:**
    - Once the cake is completely cooled, drizzle the whiskey glaze over the top, allowing it to drip down the sides.
    - Garnish with toasted pecans or walnuts and an additional drizzle of honey if desired.
5. **Serve:**
    - Slice and serve the cake at room temperature. It pairs wonderfully with coffee or a glass of whiskey.

Tips:

- **Whiskey:** Choose a whiskey that you enjoy drinking, as the flavor will come through in the cake. Bourbon or rye whiskey works well.
- **Honey:** Use high-quality honey for the best flavor.
- **Storage:** The cake can be stored in an airtight container at room temperature for up to 3 days or refrigerated for up to a week. It can also be frozen for up to 2 months; thaw in the refrigerator before serving.

Whiskey and Honey Cake is a rich and indulgent dessert with a unique flavor profile. Enjoy this delicious treat for a special occasion or a comforting dessert!

Butterscotch Cake

Ingredients:

For the Cake:

- 1 3/4 cups (220g) all-purpose flour
- 1 1/2 teaspoons baking powder
- 1/2 teaspoon baking soda
- 1/4 teaspoon salt
- 1/2 cup (115g) unsalted butter, softened
- 1 cup (200g) granulated sugar
- 1/2 cup (100g) packed brown sugar
- 2 large eggs
- 1 teaspoon vanilla extract
- 1 cup (240ml) buttermilk or milk
- 1/2 cup (120ml) butterscotch sauce (store-bought or homemade)

For the Butterscotch Frosting (optional):

- 1/2 cup (115g) unsalted butter, softened
- 1 cup (225g) packed brown sugar
- 1/4 cup (60ml) heavy cream
- 1 1/2 cups (190g) powdered sugar
- 1 teaspoon vanilla extract

For Garnish (optional):

- Additional butterscotch sauce
- Chopped nuts (such as pecans or walnuts)

Instructions:

1. **Prepare the Cake:**
   - Preheat your oven to 350°F (175°C). Grease and flour an 8-inch (20cm) round cake pan or line it with parchment paper.
   - In a medium bowl, whisk together the flour, baking powder, baking soda, and salt. Set aside.
   - In a large bowl, cream together the softened butter, granulated sugar, and brown sugar until light and fluffy.
   - Beat in the eggs one at a time, mixing well after each addition.
   - Stir in the vanilla extract.
   - Gradually add the dry ingredients to the wet mixture, alternating with the buttermilk (or milk). Begin and end with the flour mixture. Mix until just combined and smooth.
   - Gently fold in the butterscotch sauce.
   - Pour the batter into the prepared cake pan and smooth the top with a spatula.
2. **Bake the Cake:**

- Bake in the preheated oven for 30-35 minutes, or until a toothpick inserted into the center comes out clean and the cake is golden brown.
- Allow the cake to cool in the pan for 10 minutes, then transfer to a wire rack to cool completely.

3. **Prepare the Butterscotch Frosting (optional):**
   - In a medium saucepan, melt the butter over medium heat. Stir in the brown sugar and cook for 2-3 minutes, until the mixture starts to bubble.
   - Remove from heat and gradually whisk in the heavy cream until smooth.
   - Allow the mixture to cool slightly, then gradually beat in the powdered sugar and vanilla extract until the frosting is smooth and spreadable.
4. **Assemble and Garnish:**
   - Once the cake is completely cooled, spread the butterscotch frosting evenly over the top and sides of the cake, if using.
   - Garnish with additional butterscotch sauce and chopped nuts if desired.
5. **Serve:**
   - Slice and serve the cake at room temperature. It pairs beautifully with a cup of coffee or tea.

Tips:

- **Butterscotch Sauce:** You can use store-bought butterscotch sauce or make your own. If making from scratch, let it cool before mixing into the batter.
- **Frosting Consistency:** Adjust the consistency of the frosting by adding more powdered sugar if too thin or a bit more cream if too thick.
- **Storage:** The cake can be stored in an airtight container at room temperature for up to 3 days or refrigerated for up to a week. It can also be frozen for up to 2 months; thaw in the refrigerator before serving.

Butterscotch Cake is a rich and comforting dessert with a delightful caramel flavor. Enjoy this sweet treat for any special occasion or as a decadent indulgence!

Pear and Ginger Cake

Ingredients:

For the Cake:

- 1 1/2 cups (190g) all-purpose flour
- 1 1/2 teaspoons baking powder
- 1/2 teaspoon baking soda
- 1/4 teaspoon salt
- 1 teaspoon ground ginger
- 1/2 teaspoon ground cinnamon
- 1/4 teaspoon ground nutmeg (optional)
- 1/2 cup (115g) unsalted butter, softened
- 1/2 cup (100g) granulated sugar
- 1/2 cup (100g) packed brown sugar
- 2 large eggs
- 1 teaspoon vanilla extract
- 1/2 cup (120ml) buttermilk or milk
- 2 cups (about 2 medium) peeled and diced pears (such as Bartlett or Anjou)
- 1/4 cup (60ml) finely chopped crystallized ginger (optional, for extra ginger flavor)

For the Glaze (optional):

- 1 cup (120g) powdered sugar
- 2-3 tablespoons pear juice or milk
- 1/2 teaspoon vanilla extract

Instructions:

1. **Prepare the Cake:**
   - Preheat your oven to 350°F (175°C). Grease and flour an 8-inch (20cm) round cake pan or line it with parchment paper.
   - In a medium bowl, whisk together the flour, baking powder, baking soda, salt, ground ginger, cinnamon, and nutmeg (if using). Set aside.
   - In a large bowl, cream together the softened butter, granulated sugar, and brown sugar until light and fluffy.
   - Beat in the eggs one at a time, mixing well after each addition.
   - Stir in the vanilla extract.
   - Gradually add the dry ingredients to the wet mixture, alternating with the buttermilk (or milk). Begin and end with the flour mixture. Mix until just combined and smooth.
   - Gently fold in the diced pears and chopped crystallized ginger (if using).
   - Pour the batter into the prepared cake pan and smooth the top with a spatula.
2. **Bake the Cake:**
   - Bake in the preheated oven for 30-35 minutes, or until a toothpick inserted into the center comes out clean and the cake is golden brown.

- Allow the cake to cool in the pan for 10 minutes, then transfer to a wire rack to cool completely.
3. **Prepare the Glaze (optional):**
    - In a small bowl, whisk together the powdered sugar, pear juice or milk, and vanilla extract until smooth. Adjust the consistency with more juice or milk if needed.
4. **Assemble and Serve:**
    - Once the cake is completely cooled, drizzle the glaze over the top if using.
    - Slice and serve the cake at room temperature. It pairs wonderfully with a cup of tea or coffee.

Tips:

- **Pears:** Use ripe but firm pears so that they hold their shape during baking. Avoid overripe pears as they can become too mushy.
- **Crystallized Ginger:** Adding crystallized ginger will intensify the ginger flavor and provide a bit of extra texture. You can adjust the amount to your taste.
- **Storage:** The cake can be stored in an airtight container at room temperature for up to 3 days or refrigerated for up to a week. It can also be frozen for up to 2 months; thaw in the refrigerator before serving.

Pear and Ginger Cake is a delightful combination of fruity and spicy flavors that create a wonderfully moist and flavorful cake. Enjoy this comforting dessert for any occasion!

Bumbleberry Cake

Ingredients:

For the Cake:

- 1 1/2 cups (190g) all-purpose flour
- 1 1/2 teaspoons baking powder
- 1/2 teaspoon baking soda
- 1/4 teaspoon salt
- 1/2 teaspoon ground cinnamon (optional)
- 1/2 cup (115g) unsalted butter, softened
- 1 cup (200g) granulated sugar
- 2 large eggs
- 1 teaspoon vanilla extract
- 1/2 cup (120ml) buttermilk or milk
- 2 cups (about 300g) mixed berries (such as blueberries, raspberries, blackberries, and chopped strawberries)
- 1 tablespoon all-purpose flour (for tossing with berries)

For the Streusel Topping (optional):

- 1/2 cup (60g) all-purpose flour
- 1/4 cup (50g) granulated sugar
- 1/4 cup (50g) unsalted butter, cold and cut into small pieces
- 1/2 teaspoon ground cinnamon

For the Glaze (optional):

- 1 cup (120g) powdered sugar
- 2-3 tablespoons milk or lemon juice
- 1/2 teaspoon vanilla extract

Instructions:

1. **Prepare the Cake:**
    - Preheat your oven to 350°F (175°C). Grease and flour an 8-inch (20cm) round cake pan or line it with parchment paper.
    - In a medium bowl, whisk together the flour, baking powder, baking soda, salt, and cinnamon (if using). Set aside.
    - In a large bowl, cream together the softened butter and granulated sugar until light and fluffy.
    - Beat in the eggs one at a time, mixing well after each addition.
    - Stir in the vanilla extract.
    - Gradually add the dry ingredients to the wet mixture, alternating with the buttermilk (or milk). Begin and end with the flour mixture. Mix until just combined and smooth.

- In a small bowl, toss the mixed berries with 1 tablespoon of flour to coat them. This helps prevent the berries from sinking to the bottom of the cake.
- Gently fold the berries into the cake batter.
- Pour the batter into the prepared cake pan and smooth the top with a spatula.
2. **Prepare the Streusel Topping (optional):**
    - In a small bowl, mix together the flour, sugar, and cinnamon. Cut in the cold butter using a pastry blender or your fingers until the mixture resembles coarse crumbs.
    - Sprinkle the streusel topping evenly over the cake batter before baking.
3. **Bake the Cake:**
    - Bake in the preheated oven for 30-35 minutes, or until a toothpick inserted into the center comes out clean and the cake is golden brown.
    - Allow the cake to cool in the pan for 10 minutes, then transfer to a wire rack to cool completely.
4. **Prepare the Glaze (optional):**
    - In a small bowl, whisk together the powdered sugar, milk or lemon juice, and vanilla extract until smooth. Adjust the consistency with more milk or lemon juice if needed.
5. **Assemble and Serve:**
    - Once the cake is completely cooled, drizzle the glaze over the top if using.
    - Slice and serve the cake at room temperature. It pairs beautifully with a cup of tea or coffee.

Tips:

- **Berry Selection:** Feel free to use any combination of berries you like. Fresh or frozen berries work well, but if using frozen berries, do not thaw them before adding to the batter.
- **Streusel Topping:** The streusel adds a nice crunchy texture and extra sweetness. If you prefer a simpler cake, you can skip this step.
- **Storage:** The cake can be stored in an airtight container at room temperature for up to 3 days or refrigerated for up to a week. It can also be frozen for up to 2 months; thaw in the refrigerator before serving.

Bumbleberry Cake is a deliciously fruity and colorful dessert that highlights the best of berry season. Enjoy this vibrant treat with friends and family or as a special indulgence for yourself!

Chocolate Mint Cake

Ingredients:

For the Chocolate Cake:

- 1 3/4 cups (220g) all-purpose flour
- 1 1/2 teaspoons baking powder
- 1/2 teaspoon baking soda
- 1/4 teaspoon salt
- 3/4 cup (65g) unsweetened cocoa powder
- 1/2 cup (115g) unsalted butter, softened
- 1 cup (200g) granulated sugar
- 1/2 cup (100g) packed brown sugar
- 2 large eggs
- 1 teaspoon vanilla extract
- 1 cup (240ml) buttermilk or milk
- 1/2 cup (120ml) hot water

For the Mint Frosting:

- 1 cup (230g) unsalted butter, softened
- 3 1/2 cups (440g) powdered sugar
- 1/4 cup (60ml) heavy cream
- 1 teaspoon peppermint extract
- A few drops of green food coloring (optional)

For the Chocolate Ganache (optional):

- 1 cup (175g) semisweet chocolate chips
- 1/2 cup (120ml) heavy cream

For Garnish (optional):

- Fresh mint leaves
- Crushed chocolate mint candies or chocolate shavings

Instructions:

1. **Prepare the Chocolate Cake:**
    - Preheat your oven to 350°F (175°C). Grease and flour two 8-inch (20cm) round cake pans or line them with parchment paper.
    - In a medium bowl, whisk together the flour, baking powder, baking soda, salt, and cocoa powder. Set aside.
    - In a large bowl, cream together the softened butter, granulated sugar, and brown sugar until light and fluffy.
    - Beat in the eggs one at a time, mixing well after each addition.
    - Stir in the vanilla extract.

- Gradually add the dry ingredients to the wet mixture, alternating with the buttermilk (or milk). Begin and end with the flour mixture. Mix until just combined.
- Stir in the hot water until the batter is smooth and well combined.
- Divide the batter evenly between the prepared cake pans and smooth the tops with a spatula.

2. **Bake the Cake:**
   - Bake in the preheated oven for 30-35 minutes, or until a toothpick inserted into the center comes out clean and the cakes are set.
   - Allow the cakes to cool in the pans for 10 minutes, then transfer to a wire rack to cool completely.
3. **Prepare the Mint Frosting:**
   - In a large bowl, beat the softened butter until creamy.
   - Gradually add the powdered sugar, 1 cup at a time, mixing well after each addition.
   - Add the heavy cream and peppermint extract. Beat until smooth and fluffy. If desired, add a few drops of green food coloring to achieve a minty green color.
4. **Prepare the Chocolate Ganache (optional):**
   - In a heatproof bowl, combine the chocolate chips and heavy cream.
   - Microwave in 30-second intervals, stirring after each, until the chocolate is melted and smooth. Let cool slightly before using.
5. **Assemble the Cake:**
   - Place one layer of the cooled chocolate cake on a serving plate or cake stand.
   - Spread a layer of mint frosting over the top.
   - Place the second layer of cake on top and spread the remaining mint frosting evenly over the top and sides of the cake.
6. **Add the Ganache (optional):**
   - Pour the chocolate ganache over the top of the cake, allowing it to drip down the sides.
7. **Garnish and Serve:**
   - Garnish with fresh mint leaves and crushed chocolate mint candies or chocolate shavings if desired.
   - Slice and serve the cake at room temperature.

Tips:

- **Mint Extract:** Use pure peppermint extract for the best flavor. Adjust the amount to taste if you prefer a stronger or milder mint flavor.
- **Ganache:** Allow the ganache to cool slightly before pouring over the cake to prevent it from being too runny.
- **Storage:** The cake can be stored in an airtight container at room temperature for up to 3 days or refrigerated for up to a week. It can also be frozen for up to 2 months; thaw in the refrigerator before serving.

Chocolate Mint Cake is a luscious and flavorful dessert that perfectly balances the richness of chocolate with the refreshing zing of mint. Enjoy this delightful treat for any occasion!

Coconut Pineapple Cake

Ingredients:

For the Cake:

- 1 1/2 cups (190g) all-purpose flour
- 1 1/2 teaspoons baking powder
- 1/2 teaspoon baking soda
- 1/4 teaspoon salt
- 1/2 cup (115g) unsalted butter, softened
- 1 cup (200g) granulated sugar
- 1/2 cup (100g) packed brown sugar
- 2 large eggs
- 1 teaspoon vanilla extract
- 1 cup (240ml) crushed pineapple, drained (reserve juice)
- 1/2 cup (120ml) buttermilk or milk
- 1/2 cup (40g) shredded coconut (sweetened or unsweetened)

For the Coconut Frosting:

- 1 cup (230g) unsalted butter, softened
- 3 1/2 cups (440g) powdered sugar
- 1/4 cup (60ml) heavy cream
- 1 teaspoon vanilla extract
- 1/2 cup (40g) shredded coconut, toasted

For Garnish (optional):

- Additional toasted coconut
- Pineapple slices
- Maraschino cherries

Instructions:

1. **Prepare the Cake:**
    - Preheat your oven to 350°F (175°C). Grease and flour two 8-inch (20cm) round cake pans or line them with parchment paper.
    - In a medium bowl, whisk together the flour, baking powder, baking soda, and salt. Set aside.
    - In a large bowl, cream together the softened butter, granulated sugar, and brown sugar until light and fluffy.
    - Beat in the eggs one at a time, mixing well after each addition.
    - Stir in the vanilla extract.
    - Gradually add the dry ingredients to the wet mixture, alternating with the buttermilk (or milk). Begin and end with the flour mixture. Mix until just combined.

- Gently fold in the crushed pineapple (with some juice), and shredded coconut.
- Divide the batter evenly between the prepared cake pans and smooth the tops with a spatula.

2. **Bake the Cake:**
   - Bake in the preheated oven for 30-35 minutes, or until a toothpick inserted into the center comes out clean and the cakes are golden brown.
   - Allow the cakes to cool in the pans for 10 minutes, then transfer to a wire rack to cool completely.

3. **Prepare the Coconut Frosting:**
   - In a large bowl, beat the softened butter until creamy.
   - Gradually add the powdered sugar, 1 cup at a time, mixing well after each addition.
   - Add the heavy cream and vanilla extract, and beat until smooth and fluffy.
   - Gently fold in the toasted shredded coconut.

4. **Assemble and Garnish:**
   - Once the cakes are completely cooled, place one layer on a serving plate or cake stand.
   - Spread a layer of coconut frosting over the top.
   - Place the second layer of cake on top and spread the remaining frosting evenly over the top and sides of the cake.
   - Garnish with additional toasted coconut, pineapple slices, and maraschino cherries if desired.

5. **Serve:**
   - Slice and serve the cake at room temperature. It pairs wonderfully with a tropical drink or a cup of tea.

Tips:

- **Pineapple:** Make sure to drain the pineapple well to avoid excess moisture in the batter.
- **Toasting Coconut:** Toasting the coconut adds extra flavor and texture. Simply spread it out on a baking sheet and bake at 350°F (175°C) for 5-7 minutes, stirring occasionally, until golden brown.
- **Storage:** The cake can be stored in an airtight container at room temperature for up to 3 days or refrigerated for up to a week. It can also be frozen for up to 2 months; thaw in the refrigerator before serving.

Coconut Pineapple Cake is a delicious and tropical treat that brings a taste of paradise to your dessert table. Enjoy this delightful cake with family and friends!

Strawberry Rhubarb Cake

Ingredients:

For the Cake:

- 1 1/2 cups (190g) all-purpose flour
- 1 1/2 teaspoons baking powder
- 1/2 teaspoon baking soda
- 1/4 teaspoon salt
- 1/2 cup (115g) unsalted butter, softened
- 1 cup (200g) granulated sugar
- 2 large eggs
- 1 teaspoon vanilla extract
- 1/2 cup (120ml) buttermilk or milk
- 1 cup (150g) diced fresh strawberries
- 1 cup (150g) diced rhubarb (fresh or frozen, thawed and drained)

For the Streusel Topping (optional):

- 1/3 cup (40g) all-purpose flour
- 1/4 cup (50g) granulated sugar
- 1/4 cup (50g) unsalted butter, cold and cut into small pieces
- 1/2 teaspoon ground cinnamon

For the Glaze (optional):

- 1 cup (120g) powdered sugar
- 2-3 tablespoons milk or lemon juice
- 1/2 teaspoon vanilla extract

Instructions:

1. **Prepare the Cake:**
   - Preheat your oven to 350°F (175°C). Grease and flour a 9-inch (23cm) round cake pan or line it with parchment paper.
   - In a medium bowl, whisk together the flour, baking powder, baking soda, and salt. Set aside.
   - In a large bowl, cream together the softened butter and granulated sugar until light and fluffy.
   - Beat in the eggs one at a time, mixing well after each addition.
   - Stir in the vanilla extract.
   - Gradually add the dry ingredients to the wet mixture, alternating with the buttermilk (or milk). Begin and end with the flour mixture. Mix until just combined and smooth.
   - Gently fold in the diced strawberries and rhubarb.

- Pour the batter into the prepared cake pan and smooth the top with a spatula.
2. **Prepare the Streusel Topping (optional):**
   - In a small bowl, mix together the flour, sugar, and cinnamon. Cut in the cold butter using a pastry blender or your fingers until the mixture resembles coarse crumbs.
   - Sprinkle the streusel topping evenly over the cake batter before baking.
3. **Bake the Cake:**
   - Bake in the preheated oven for 35-40 minutes, or until a toothpick inserted into the center comes out clean and the cake is golden brown.
   - Allow the cake to cool in the pan for 10 minutes, then transfer to a wire rack to cool completely.
4. **Prepare the Glaze (optional):**
   - In a small bowl, whisk together the powdered sugar, milk or lemon juice, and vanilla extract until smooth. Adjust the consistency with more milk or lemon juice if needed.
5. **Assemble and Serve:**
   - Once the cake is completely cooled, drizzle the glaze over the top if using.
   - Slice and serve the cake at room temperature. It pairs wonderfully with a cup of tea or coffee.

Tips:

- **Rhubarb:** If using frozen rhubarb, ensure it's fully thawed and drained to prevent excess moisture in the cake.
- **Strawberries:** You can use fresh or frozen strawberries. If using frozen, do not thaw them before adding to the batter.
- **Storage:** The cake can be stored in an airtight container at room temperature for up to 3 days or refrigerated for up to a week. It can also be frozen for up to 2 months; thaw in the refrigerator before serving.

Strawberry Rhubarb Cake offers a perfect balance of sweet and tart flavors with a lovely, moist crumb. Enjoy this charming and delicious dessert with friends and family!

Dulce de Leche Cake

Ingredients:

For the Cake:

- 1 1/2 cups (190g) all-purpose flour
- 1 1/2 teaspoons baking powder
- 1/2 teaspoon baking soda
- 1/4 teaspoon salt
- 1/2 cup (115g) unsalted butter, softened
- 1 cup (200g) granulated sugar
- 1/2 cup (100g) packed brown sugar
- 2 large eggs
- 1 teaspoon vanilla extract
- 1 cup (240ml) buttermilk or milk
- 1/2 cup (120ml) dulce de leche (store-bought or homemade)

For the Dulce de Leche Frosting:

- 1 cup (230g) unsalted butter, softened
- 2 cups (240g) powdered sugar
- 1/2 cup (120ml) dulce de leche
- 1 teaspoon vanilla extract
- A pinch of salt

For the Caramel Drizzle (optional):

- 1/2 cup (100g) granulated sugar
- 1/4 cup (60ml) heavy cream
- 1 tablespoon unsalted butter

For Garnish (optional):

- Whipped cream
- Extra dulce de leche
- Caramel shards or sea salt

Instructions:

1. **Prepare the Cake:**
    - Preheat your oven to 350°F (175°C). Grease and flour two 8-inch (20cm) round cake pans or line them with parchment paper.
    - In a medium bowl, whisk together the flour, baking powder, baking soda, and salt. Set aside.

- In a large bowl, cream together the softened butter, granulated sugar, and brown sugar until light and fluffy.
- Beat in the eggs one at a time, mixing well after each addition.
- Stir in the vanilla extract.
- Gradually add the dry ingredients to the wet mixture, alternating with the buttermilk (or milk). Begin and end with the flour mixture. Mix until just combined.
- Gently fold in the dulce de leche until evenly distributed.
- Divide the batter evenly between the prepared cake pans and smooth the tops with a spatula.

2. **Bake the Cake:**
   - Bake in the preheated oven for 30-35 minutes, or until a toothpick inserted into the center comes out clean and the cakes are golden brown.
   - Allow the cakes to cool in the pans for 10 minutes, then transfer to a wire rack to cool completely.

3. **Prepare the Dulce de Leche Frosting:**
   - In a large bowl, beat the softened butter until creamy.
   - Gradually add the powdered sugar, mixing well after each addition.
   - Add the dulce de leche, vanilla extract, and a pinch of salt. Beat until smooth and fluffy.

4. **Prepare the Caramel Drizzle (optional):**
   - In a small saucepan over medium heat, melt the sugar, stirring constantly until it turns a deep amber color.
   - Carefully add the heavy cream and butter, stirring until smooth and combined. Remove from heat and let cool slightly before using.

5. **Assemble and Frost the Cake:**
   - Once the cakes are completely cooled, place one layer on a serving plate or cake stand.
   - Spread a layer of dulce de leche frosting over the top.
   - Place the second layer on top and frost the top and sides of the cake with the remaining dulce de leche frosting.

6. **Add the Caramel Drizzle and Garnish (optional):**
   - Drizzle the caramel sauce over the top of the frosted cake.
   - Garnish with whipped cream, extra dulce de leche, and caramel shards or a sprinkle of sea salt if desired.

7. **Serve:**
   - Slice and serve the cake at room temperature. It pairs beautifully with a cup of coffee or a glass of milk.

Tips:

- **Dulce de Leche:** Store-bought dulce de leche works well, but you can also make it at home using sweetened condensed milk if you prefer.
- **Caramel Drizzle:** Be cautious when making caramel as it gets very hot. Allow it to cool slightly before drizzling over the cake.

- **Storage:** The cake can be stored in an airtight container at room temperature for up to 3 days or refrigerated for up to a week. It can also be frozen for up to 2 months; thaw in the refrigerator before serving.

Dulce de Leche Cake is a wonderfully indulgent dessert that's sure to impress. Enjoy the creamy, caramel goodness in every bite!

Maple Apple Cake

Ingredients:

For the Cake:

- 1 1/2 cups (190g) all-purpose flour
- 1 1/2 teaspoons baking powder
- 1/2 teaspoon baking soda
- 1/4 teaspoon salt
- 1/2 teaspoon ground cinnamon
- 1/4 teaspoon ground nutmeg
- 1/2 cup (115g) unsalted butter, softened
- 1 cup (200g) granulated sugar
- 1/2 cup (120ml) pure maple syrup
- 2 large eggs
- 1 teaspoon vanilla extract
- 1/2 cup (120ml) buttermilk or milk
- 1 1/2 cups (about 2 medium) peeled and diced apples (e.g., Granny Smith or Honeycrisp)

For the Maple Glaze (optional):

- 1 cup (120g) powdered sugar
- 2-3 tablespoons pure maple syrup
- 1/2 teaspoon vanilla extract

For Garnish (optional):

- Additional maple syrup
- Sliced apples
- Chopped nuts (such as walnuts or pecans)

Instructions:

1. **Prepare the Cake:**
    - Preheat your oven to 350°F (175°C). Grease and flour a 9-inch (23cm) round cake pan or line it with parchment paper.
    - In a medium bowl, whisk together the flour, baking powder, baking soda, salt, cinnamon, and nutmeg. Set aside.
    - In a large bowl, cream together the softened butter and granulated sugar until light and fluffy.
    - Beat in the eggs one at a time, mixing well after each addition.
    - Stir in the maple syrup and vanilla extract.
    - Gradually add the dry ingredients to the wet mixture, alternating with the buttermilk (or milk). Begin and end with the flour mixture. Mix until just combined.

- Gently fold in the diced apples.
- Pour the batter into the prepared cake pan and smooth the top with a spatula.

2. **Bake the Cake:**
    - Bake in the preheated oven for 35-40 minutes, or until a toothpick inserted into the center comes out clean and the cake is golden brown.
    - Allow the cake to cool in the pan for 10 minutes, then transfer to a wire rack to cool completely.
3. **Prepare the Maple Glaze (optional):**
    - In a small bowl, whisk together the powdered sugar, maple syrup, and vanilla extract until smooth. Adjust the consistency with more maple syrup if needed.
4. **Assemble and Garnish:**
    - Once the cake is completely cooled, drizzle the maple glaze over the top if using.
    - Garnish with additional maple syrup, sliced apples, and chopped nuts if desired.
5. **Serve:**
    - Slice and serve the cake at room temperature. It pairs beautifully with a cup of coffee or tea.

Tips:

- **Apples:** Use firm apples that hold their shape well during baking. Avoid using overly soft apples as they may turn mushy.
- **Maple Syrup:** Use pure maple syrup for the best flavor. It adds a rich, natural sweetness to the cake.
- **Storage:** The cake can be stored in an airtight container at room temperature for up to 3 days or refrigerated for up to a week. It can also be frozen for up to 2 months; thaw in the refrigerator before serving.

Maple Apple Cake is a wonderful way to enjoy the flavors of fall with its comforting blend of maple and apple. Enjoy this tasty and aromatic cake with friends and family!

Pecan Pie Cake

Ingredients:

For the Cake:

- 1 1/2 cups (190g) all-purpose flour
- 1 1/2 teaspoons baking powder
- 1/2 teaspoon baking soda
- 1/4 teaspoon salt
- 1/2 teaspoon ground cinnamon
- 1/2 cup (115g) unsalted butter, softened
- 1 cup (200g) granulated sugar
- 1/2 cup (100g) packed brown sugar
- 2 large eggs
- 1 teaspoon vanilla extract
- 1/2 cup (120ml) sour cream or Greek yogurt
- 1/2 cup (120ml) buttermilk or milk

For the Pecan Pie Topping:

- 1/2 cup (115g) unsalted butter
- 1 cup (200g) packed brown sugar
- 1/2 cup (120ml) light corn syrup or golden syrup
- 1 large egg
- 1 teaspoon vanilla extract
- 1 1/2 cups (180g) pecan halves

For Garnish (optional):

- Whipped cream
- Additional pecans

Instructions:

1. **Prepare the Cake:**
   - Preheat your oven to 350°F (175°C). Grease and flour a 9-inch (23cm) round cake pan or line it with parchment paper.
   - In a medium bowl, whisk together the flour, baking powder, baking soda, salt, and cinnamon. Set aside.
   - In a large bowl, cream together the softened butter, granulated sugar, and brown sugar until light and fluffy.
   - Beat in the eggs one at a time, mixing well after each addition.
   - Stir in the vanilla extract.

- Gradually add the dry ingredients to the wet mixture, alternating with the sour cream (or Greek yogurt) and buttermilk (or milk). Begin and end with the flour mixture. Mix until just combined and smooth.
- Pour the batter into the prepared cake pan and smooth the top with a spatula.

2. **Prepare the Pecan Pie Topping:**
    - In a medium saucepan over medium heat, melt the butter.
    - Stir in the brown sugar and corn syrup (or golden syrup) and cook until the mixture is smooth and starts to bubble.
    - Remove from heat and let cool slightly.
    - Whisk in the egg and vanilla extract until well combined.
    - Stir in the pecan halves.
3. **Add the Topping and Bake:**
    - Spoon the pecan pie topping over the cake batter, spreading it evenly.
    - Bake in the preheated oven for 40-45 minutes, or until a toothpick inserted into the center of the cake comes out clean and the topping is bubbly and caramelized.
    - Allow the cake to cool in the pan for 15 minutes, then transfer to a wire rack to cool completely.
4. **Garnish and Serve:**
    - Once the cake is completely cooled, garnish with whipped cream and additional pecans if desired.
    - Slice and serve the cake at room temperature. It pairs beautifully with a cup of coffee or tea.

Tips:

- **Pecans:** Toasting the pecans before adding them to the topping can enhance their flavor.
- **Topping:** If the topping starts to brown too quickly during baking, cover the cake loosely with aluminum foil.
- **Storage:** The cake can be stored in an airtight container at room temperature for up to 3 days or refrigerated for up to a week. It can also be frozen for up to 2 months; thaw in the refrigerator before serving.

Pecan Pie Cake brings together the best of both worlds—cake and pecan pie—into one irresistible dessert. Enjoy this sweet, nutty treat with family and friends!

Mango Coconut Cake

Ingredients:

For the Cake:

- 1 1/2 cups (190g) all-purpose flour
- 1 1/2 teaspoons baking powder
- 1/2 teaspoon baking soda
- 1/4 teaspoon salt
- 1/2 cup (115g) unsalted butter, softened
- 1 cup (200g) granulated sugar
- 2 large eggs
- 1 teaspoon vanilla extract
- 1/2 cup (120ml) coconut milk
- 1/2 cup (120ml) mango puree (store-bought or homemade)
- 1/2 cup (40g) shredded coconut (sweetened or unsweetened)

For the Mango Coconut Frosting:

- 1 cup (230g) unsalted butter, softened
- 2 1/2 cups (300g) powdered sugar
- 1/4 cup (60ml) coconut milk
- 1/4 cup (60ml) mango puree
- 1 teaspoon vanilla extract
- A pinch of salt
- 1/2 cup (40g) shredded coconut (for garnish)

For Garnish (optional):

- Fresh mango slices
- Toasted coconut
- Mint leaves

Instructions:

1. **Prepare the Cake:**
    - Preheat your oven to 350°F (175°C). Grease and flour two 8-inch (20cm) round cake pans or line them with parchment paper.
    - In a medium bowl, whisk together the flour, baking powder, baking soda, and salt. Set aside.
    - In a large bowl, cream together the softened butter and granulated sugar until light and fluffy.
    - Beat in the eggs one at a time, mixing well after each addition.
    - Stir in the vanilla extract.

- Gradually add the dry ingredients to the wet mixture, alternating with the coconut milk and mango puree. Begin and end with the flour mixture. Mix until just combined and smooth.
- Gently fold in the shredded coconut.
- Divide the batter evenly between the prepared cake pans and smooth the tops with a spatula.

2. **Bake the Cake:**
    - Bake in the preheated oven for 30-35 minutes, or until a toothpick inserted into the center comes out clean and the cakes are golden brown.
    - Allow the cakes to cool in the pans for 10 minutes, then transfer to a wire rack to cool completely.

3. **Prepare the Mango Coconut Frosting:**
    - In a large bowl, beat the softened butter until creamy.
    - Gradually add the powdered sugar, mixing well after each addition.
    - Add the coconut milk, mango puree, vanilla extract, and a pinch of salt. Beat until smooth and fluffy.

4. **Assemble and Frost the Cake:**
    - Once the cakes are completely cooled, place one layer on a serving plate or cake stand.
    - Spread a layer of mango coconut frosting over the top.
    - Place the second layer on top and frost the top and sides of the cake with the remaining frosting.
    - Garnish with shredded coconut, fresh mango slices, toasted coconut, and mint leaves if desired.

5. **Serve:**
    - Slice and serve the cake at room temperature. It pairs wonderfully with a tropical drink or a cup of tea.

Tips:

- **Mango Puree:** You can use store-bought mango puree or make your own by blending ripe mangoes until smooth.
- **Coconut Milk:** Use full-fat coconut milk for a richer flavor and creamier texture.
- **Shredded Coconut:** Toasting the shredded coconut can enhance its flavor and add extra texture.

Mango Coconut Cake is a tropical treat that brings a refreshing and exotic twist to your dessert table. Enjoy this moist and flavorful cake with friends and family!

Lemon Lavender Cake

Ingredients:

For the Cake:

- 1 1/2 cups (190g) all-purpose flour
- 1 1/2 teaspoons baking powder
- 1/2 teaspoon baking soda
- 1/4 teaspoon salt
- 1/4 cup (60ml) milk
- 1/4 cup (60ml) boiling water
- 1 tablespoon dried culinary lavender buds
- 1/2 cup (115g) unsalted butter, softened
- 1 cup (200g) granulated sugar
- 2 large eggs
- 1 tablespoon lemon zest (from about 1 lemon)
- 2 tablespoons fresh lemon juice
- 1/2 cup (120ml) buttermilk or plain yogurt

For the Lemon Lavender Frosting:

- 1 cup (230g) unsalted butter, softened
- 3-4 cups (360-480g) powdered sugar, sifted
- 2 tablespoons fresh lemon juice
- 1 tablespoon lemon zest
- 1-2 tablespoons milk or cream (if needed for consistency)
- 1 teaspoon dried culinary lavender buds (optional, for garnish)

For Garnish (optional):

- Lemon zest
- Fresh lavender sprigs
- Lemon slices

Instructions:

1. **Prepare the Cake:**
    - Preheat your oven to 350°F (175°C). Grease and flour two 8-inch (20cm) round cake pans or line them with parchment paper.
    - In a small bowl, combine the milk and boiling water. Add the dried lavender buds and let steep for about 5 minutes. Strain out the lavender and set the infused milk aside.
    - In a medium bowl, whisk together the flour, baking powder, baking soda, and salt. Set aside.

- In a large bowl, cream together the softened butter and granulated sugar until light and fluffy.
- Beat in the eggs one at a time, mixing well after each addition.
- Stir in the lemon zest and lemon juice.
- Gradually add the dry ingredients to the wet mixture, alternating with the infused milk and buttermilk (or yogurt). Begin and end with the flour mixture. Mix until just combined and smooth.
- Divide the batter evenly between the prepared cake pans and smooth the tops with a spatula.

2. **Bake the Cake:**
   - Bake in the preheated oven for 25-30 minutes, or until a toothpick inserted into the center comes out clean and the cakes are golden brown.
   - Allow the cakes to cool in the pans for 10 minutes, then transfer to a wire rack to cool completely.

3. **Prepare the Lemon Lavender Frosting:**
   - In a large bowl, beat the softened butter until creamy.
   - Gradually add the powdered sugar, mixing well after each addition.
   - Add the lemon juice, lemon zest, and mix until smooth. Adjust the consistency with milk or cream if needed.
   - If desired, you can add a teaspoon of dried lavender buds for additional flavor and garnish.

4. **Assemble and Frost the Cake:**
   - Once the cakes are completely cooled, place one layer on a serving plate or cake stand.
   - Spread a layer of lemon lavender frosting over the top.
   - Place the second layer on top and frost the top and sides of the cake with the remaining frosting.
   - Garnish with additional lemon zest, fresh lavender sprigs, and lemon slices if desired.

5. **Serve:**
   - Slice and serve the cake at room temperature. It pairs wonderfully with tea or a light, citrusy beverage.

Tips:

- **Lavender:** Ensure you use culinary lavender that is safe for consumption, as some lavender varieties are treated with chemicals.
- **Lemon Zest:** Use a microplane or fine grater to get finely grated lemon zest for the best flavor.
- **Infused Milk:** For a more pronounced lavender flavor, you can increase the amount of dried lavender buds slightly.

Lemon Lavender Cake offers a unique blend of bright lemon flavor and delicate lavender, making it a sophisticated and refreshing dessert. Enjoy this elegant treat with a cup of tea or at your next special occasion!

Pumpkin Caramel Cake

Ingredients:

For the Cake:

- 1 1/2 cups (190g) all-purpose flour
- 1 1/2 teaspoons baking powder
- 1/2 teaspoon baking soda
- 1/4 teaspoon salt
- 1 teaspoon ground cinnamon
- 1/2 teaspoon ground nutmeg
- 1/2 teaspoon ground ginger
- 1/2 teaspoon ground cloves
- 1/2 cup (115g) unsalted butter, softened
- 1 cup (200g) granulated sugar
- 1/2 cup (100g) packed brown sugar
- 2 large eggs
- 1 cup (240ml) canned pumpkin puree
- 1/2 cup (120ml) buttermilk or milk
- 1 teaspoon vanilla extract

For the Caramel Sauce:

- 1 cup (200g) granulated sugar
- 6 tablespoons unsalted butter
- 1/2 cup (120ml) heavy cream
- 1/4 teaspoon salt
- 1 teaspoon vanilla extract

For the Frosting (optional):

- 1/2 cup (115g) unsalted butter, softened
- 1 cup (120g) powdered sugar
- 2 tablespoons caramel sauce (from above)
- 1/2 teaspoon vanilla extract

For Garnish (optional):

- Extra caramel sauce
- Crushed pecans or walnuts
- Whipped cream

Instructions:

1. **Prepare the Cake:**

- Preheat your oven to 350°F (175°C). Grease and flour two 8-inch (20cm) round cake pans or line them with parchment paper.
- In a medium bowl, whisk together the flour, baking powder, baking soda, salt, cinnamon, nutmeg, ginger, and cloves. Set aside.
- In a large bowl, cream together the softened butter, granulated sugar, and brown sugar until light and fluffy.
- Beat in the eggs one at a time, mixing well after each addition.
- Stir in the pumpkin puree and vanilla extract.
- Gradually add the dry ingredients to the wet mixture, alternating with the buttermilk (or milk). Begin and end with the flour mixture. Mix until just combined and smooth.
- Divide the batter evenly between the prepared cake pans and smooth the tops with a spatula.

2. **Bake the Cake:**
   - Bake in the preheated oven for 30-35 minutes, or until a toothpick inserted into the center comes out clean and the cakes are golden brown.
   - Allow the cakes to cool in the pans for 10 minutes, then transfer to a wire rack to cool completely.

3. **Prepare the Caramel Sauce:**
   - In a medium saucepan over medium heat, melt the granulated sugar, stirring constantly until it turns a deep amber color.
   - Carefully add the butter and stir until melted and combined.
   - Slowly add the heavy cream, stirring constantly until the mixture is smooth.
   - Remove from heat and stir in the salt and vanilla extract. Let the caramel sauce cool to room temperature.

4. **Prepare the Frosting (optional):**
   - In a medium bowl, beat the softened butter until creamy.
   - Gradually add the powdered sugar, mixing well after each addition.
   - Mix in 2 tablespoons of the cooled caramel sauce and vanilla extract until smooth and fluffy. Adjust the consistency with more powdered sugar if needed.

5. **Assemble and Frost the Cake:**
   - Once the cakes are completely cooled, place one layer on a serving plate or cake stand.
   - Spread a layer of frosting over the top (if using) or drizzle with a bit of caramel sauce.
   - Place the second layer on top and frost the top and sides of the cake with the remaining frosting (if using).
   - Drizzle additional caramel sauce over the top and garnish with crushed pecans or walnuts if desired.

6. **Serve:**
   - Slice and serve the cake at room temperature. It pairs beautifully with a cup of coffee or tea.

Tips:

- **Pumpkin Puree:** Use canned pumpkin puree for convenience, but make sure it's 100% pure pumpkin and not pumpkin pie filling.
- **Caramel Sauce:** Be cautious when making caramel as it gets very hot. Let it cool to a pourable consistency before using.
- **Storage:** The cake can be stored in an airtight container at room temperature for up to 3 days or refrigerated for up to a week. It can also be frozen for up to 2 months; thaw in the refrigerator before serving.

Pumpkin Caramel Cake is a rich and comforting dessert that combines the best flavors of autumn. Enjoy this sweet, spiced cake with its luscious caramel topping!

Maple Carrot Cake

Ingredients:

For the Cake:

- 1 1/2 cups (190g) all-purpose flour
- 1 teaspoon baking powder
- 1/2 teaspoon baking soda
- 1/4 teaspoon salt
- 1 teaspoon ground cinnamon
- 1/2 teaspoon ground nutmeg
- 1/2 teaspoon ground ginger
- 1/2 cup (115g) unsalted butter, softened
- 1/2 cup (100g) granulated sugar
- 1/2 cup (100g) packed brown sugar
- 2 large eggs
- 1/2 cup (120ml) pure maple syrup
- 1 cup (240ml) finely grated carrots (about 2 medium carrots)
- 1/2 cup (120ml) vegetable oil
- 1/2 cup (80g) chopped walnuts or pecans (optional)
- 1/2 cup (80g) raisins (optional)

For the Maple Cream Cheese Frosting:

- 8 oz (225g) cream cheese, softened
- 1/2 cup (115g) unsalted butter, softened
- 2-3 cups (240-360g) powdered sugar, sifted
- 1/4 cup (60ml) pure maple syrup
- 1 teaspoon vanilla extract

For Garnish (optional):

- Additional chopped walnuts or pecans
- Maple syrup drizzle
- Carrot shavings

Instructions:

1. **Prepare the Cake:**
    - Preheat your oven to 350°F (175°C). Grease and flour two 8-inch (20cm) round cake pans or line them with parchment paper.
    - In a medium bowl, whisk together the flour, baking powder, baking soda, salt, cinnamon, nutmeg, and ginger. Set aside.
    - In a large bowl, cream together the softened butter, granulated sugar, and brown sugar until light and fluffy.

- Beat in the eggs one at a time, mixing well after each addition.
- Stir in the pure maple syrup.
- Gradually add the dry ingredients to the wet mixture, alternating with the vegetable oil. Begin and end with the flour mixture. Mix until just combined.
- Fold in the finely grated carrots, and if using, the chopped walnuts or pecans and raisins.
- Divide the batter evenly between the prepared cake pans and smooth the tops with a spatula.

2. **Bake the Cake:**
    - Bake in the preheated oven for 30-35 minutes, or until a toothpick inserted into the center comes out clean and the cakes are golden brown.
    - Allow the cakes to cool in the pans for 10 minutes, then transfer to a wire rack to cool completely.
3. **Prepare the Maple Cream Cheese Frosting:**
    - In a large bowl, beat the softened cream cheese and butter until creamy and smooth.
    - Gradually add the powdered sugar, mixing well after each addition.
    - Beat in the pure maple syrup and vanilla extract until the frosting is smooth and fluffy.
4. **Assemble and Frost the Cake:**
    - Once the cakes are completely cooled, place one layer on a serving plate or cake stand.
    - Spread a layer of maple cream cheese frosting over the top.
    - Place the second layer on top and frost the top and sides of the cake with the remaining frosting.
    - Garnish with additional chopped walnuts or pecans, a drizzle of maple syrup, and carrot shavings if desired.
5. **Serve:**
    - Slice and serve the cake at room temperature. It pairs wonderfully with a cup of coffee or tea.

Tips:

- **Carrots:** Grate the carrots finely for a smooth texture and to ensure they blend well into the cake batter.
- **Maple Syrup:** Use pure maple syrup for the best flavor. It adds a rich, natural sweetness that complements the carrots perfectly.
- **Storage:** The cake can be stored in an airtight container in the refrigerator for up to a week. It can also be frozen for up to 2 months; thaw in the refrigerator before serving.

Maple Carrot Cake combines the classic flavors of carrot cake with a sweet maple twist, making it a delightful treat for any occasion. Enjoy this moist and flavorful cake with family and friends!

Raisin Spice Cake

Ingredients:

For the Cake:

- 1 1/2 cups (190g) all-purpose flour
- 1 teaspoon baking powder
- 1/2 teaspoon baking soda
- 1/4 teaspoon salt
- 1 teaspoon ground cinnamon
- 1/2 teaspoon ground nutmeg
- 1/2 teaspoon ground ginger
- 1/4 teaspoon ground cloves
- 1/2 cup (115g) unsalted butter, softened
- 1 cup (200g) granulated sugar
- 2 large eggs
- 1/2 cup (120ml) buttermilk or milk
- 1/2 cup (120ml) applesauce
- 1 cup (150g) raisins
- 1/2 cup (60g) chopped walnuts or pecans (optional)

For the Glaze (optional):

- 1/2 cup (60g) powdered sugar
- 2-3 tablespoons milk or cream
- 1/2 teaspoon vanilla extract

Instructions:

1. **Prepare the Cake:**
    - Preheat your oven to 350°F (175°C). Grease and flour a 9-inch (23cm) round cake pan or line it with parchment paper.
    - In a medium bowl, whisk together the flour, baking powder, baking soda, salt, cinnamon, nutmeg, ginger, and cloves. Set aside.
    - In a large bowl, cream together the softened butter and granulated sugar until light and fluffy.
    - Beat in the eggs one at a time, mixing well after each addition.
    - Stir in the applesauce.
    - Gradually add the dry ingredients to the wet mixture, alternating with the buttermilk (or milk). Begin and end with the flour mixture. Mix until just combined.
    - Fold in the raisins and chopped nuts if using.
    - Pour the batter into the prepared cake pan and smooth the top with a spatula.
2. **Bake the Cake:**

- Bake in the preheated oven for 30-35 minutes, or until a toothpick inserted into the center comes out clean and the cake is golden brown.
- Allow the cake to cool in the pan for 10 minutes, then transfer to a wire rack to cool completely.

3. **Prepare the Glaze (optional):**
   - In a small bowl, whisk together the powdered sugar, milk or cream, and vanilla extract until smooth. Adjust the consistency with more milk or powdered sugar as needed.
4. **Assemble and Glaze the Cake:**
   - Once the cake is completely cooled, drizzle the glaze over the top. Let it set before slicing.
5. **Serve:**
   - Slice and serve the cake at room temperature. It pairs wonderfully with a cup of tea or coffee.

Tips:

- **Raisins:** For extra plump raisins, soak them in hot water for 10 minutes and drain well before adding them to the batter.
- **Spices:** Adjust the amount of spices to your taste. You can also add a pinch of cardamom or allspice for extra depth of flavor.
- **Storage:** The cake can be stored in an airtight container at room temperature for up to 3 days or refrigerated for up to a week. It can also be frozen for up to 2 months; thaw in the refrigerator before serving.

Raisin Spice Cake is a comforting and flavorful dessert that's perfect for any time of year. Enjoy its rich spices and sweet raisins with your favorite beverage!

Coffee and Walnut Cake

Ingredients:

For the Cake:

- 1 3/4 cups (220g) all-purpose flour
- 1 1/2 teaspoons baking powder
- 1/2 teaspoon baking soda
- 1/4 teaspoon salt
- 1/2 cup (115g) unsalted butter, softened
- 1 cup (200g) granulated sugar
- 2 large eggs
- 1/2 cup (120ml) brewed coffee, cooled
- 1/4 cup (60ml) milk
- 1 teaspoon vanilla extract
- 1 cup (120g) chopped walnuts

For the Coffee Buttercream Frosting:

- 1/2 cup (115g) unsalted butter, softened
- 2 cups (240g) powdered sugar
- 2 tablespoons brewed coffee, cooled
- 1 tablespoon milk or cream
- 1 teaspoon vanilla extract

For Garnish (optional):

- Additional chopped walnuts
- Coffee beans
- A dusting of cocoa powder or espresso powder

Instructions:

1. **Prepare the Cake:**
    - Preheat your oven to 350°F (175°C). Grease and flour two 8-inch (20cm) round cake pans or line them with parchment paper.
    - In a medium bowl, whisk together the flour, baking powder, baking soda, and salt. Set aside.
    - In a large bowl, cream together the softened butter and granulated sugar until light and fluffy.
    - Beat in the eggs one at a time, mixing well after each addition.
    - Stir in the vanilla extract.
    - Gradually add the dry ingredients to the wet mixture, alternating with the brewed coffee and milk. Begin and end with the flour mixture. Mix until just combined.
    - Fold in the chopped walnuts.

- Divide the batter evenly between the prepared cake pans and smooth the tops with a spatula.
2. **Bake the Cake:**
    - Bake in the preheated oven for 25-30 minutes, or until a toothpick inserted into the center comes out clean and the cakes are golden brown.
    - Allow the cakes to cool in the pans for 10 minutes, then transfer to a wire rack to cool completely.
3. **Prepare the Coffee Buttercream Frosting:**
    - In a large bowl, beat the softened butter until creamy.
    - Gradually add the powdered sugar, mixing well after each addition.
    - Mix in the brewed coffee, milk or cream, and vanilla extract until the frosting is smooth and fluffy.
4. **Assemble and Frost the Cake:**
    - Once the cakes are completely cooled, place one layer on a serving plate or cake stand.
    - Spread a layer of coffee buttercream frosting over the top.
    - Place the second layer on top and frost the top and sides of the cake with the remaining frosting.
    - Garnish with additional chopped walnuts, coffee beans, or a dusting of cocoa powder if desired.
5. **Serve:**
    - Slice and serve the cake at room temperature. It pairs beautifully with a cup of coffee or tea.

Tips:

- **Coffee:** Use a strong, brewed coffee for the best flavor. You can also use espresso if you prefer a more intense coffee taste.
- **Walnuts:** Toasting the walnuts lightly before adding them to the batter can enhance their flavor.
- **Buttercream Consistency:** If the buttercream is too thick, add a bit more milk or cream to reach your desired consistency. If too thin, add more powdered sugar.

Coffee and Walnut Cake is a rich and satisfying dessert that combines the best of coffee and nuts in every bite. Enjoy this classic cake with your favorite brew or as a delightful treat for your next gathering!

Lemon Raspberry Cake

Ingredients:

For the Cake:

- 1 3/4 cups (220g) all-purpose flour
- 1 1/2 teaspoons baking powder
- 1/2 teaspoon baking soda
- 1/4 teaspoon salt
- 1/2 cup (115g) unsalted butter, softened
- 1 cup (200g) granulated sugar
- 2 large eggs
- 1/2 cup (120ml) milk
- 1/4 cup (60ml) fresh lemon juice
- 1 tablespoon lemon zest (from about 1 lemon)
- 1 teaspoon vanilla extract
- 1 cup (120g) fresh raspberries (if using frozen, thaw and drain them)

For the Lemon Glaze:

- 1 cup (120g) powdered sugar
- 2-3 tablespoons fresh lemon juice
- 1 teaspoon lemon zest

For the Lemon Raspberry Frosting:

- 1/2 cup (115g) unsalted butter, softened
- 1 cup (120g) powdered sugar
- 2 tablespoons fresh lemon juice
- 1 tablespoon lemon zest
- 1-2 tablespoons milk or cream (if needed for consistency)
- 1/2 cup (60g) fresh raspberries, mashed

For Garnish (optional):

- Additional fresh raspberries
- Lemon zest
- Mint leaves

Instructions:

1. **Prepare the Cake:**
    - Preheat your oven to 350°F (175°C). Grease and flour two 8-inch (20cm) round cake pans or line them with parchment paper.

- In a medium bowl, whisk together the flour, baking powder, baking soda, and salt. Set aside.
- In a large bowl, cream together the softened butter and granulated sugar until light and fluffy.
- Beat in the eggs one at a time, mixing well after each addition.
- Stir in the lemon juice, lemon zest, and vanilla extract.
- Gradually add the dry ingredients to the wet mixture, alternating with the milk. Begin and end with the flour mixture. Mix until just combined.
- Gently fold in the fresh raspberries.
- Divide the batter evenly between the prepared cake pans and smooth the tops with a spatula.

2. **Bake the Cake:**
    - Bake in the preheated oven for 25-30 minutes, or until a toothpick inserted into the center comes out clean and the cakes are golden brown.
    - Allow the cakes to cool in the pans for 10 minutes, then transfer to a wire rack to cool completely.

3. **Prepare the Lemon Glaze:**
    - In a small bowl, whisk together the powdered sugar, lemon juice, and lemon zest until smooth. Adjust the consistency with more lemon juice or powdered sugar as needed.

4. **Prepare the Lemon Raspberry Frosting:**
    - In a large bowl, beat the softened butter until creamy.
    - Gradually add the powdered sugar, mixing well after each addition.
    - Mix in the lemon juice and lemon zest until smooth.
    - Fold in the mashed raspberries.
    - Adjust the consistency with milk or cream if needed.

5. **Assemble and Frost the Cake:**
    - Once the cakes are completely cooled, place one layer on a serving plate or cake stand.
    - Spread a layer of lemon raspberry frosting over the top.
    - Place the second layer on top and frost the top and sides of the cake with the remaining frosting.
    - Drizzle the lemon glaze over the top of the cake, letting it drizzle down the sides.
    - Garnish with additional fresh raspberries, lemon zest, and mint leaves if desired.

6. **Serve:**
    - Slice and serve the cake at room temperature. It pairs beautifully with a cup of tea or a light, refreshing beverage.

Tips:

- **Raspberries:** Gently fold in the raspberries to avoid breaking them up too much. If using frozen raspberries, make sure to thaw and drain them well to avoid excess moisture in the batter.

- **Glaze Consistency:** The glaze should be thick enough to drizzle but thin enough to flow easily. Adjust with more lemon juice or powdered sugar as needed.
- **Frosting Consistency:** If the frosting is too thick, add a bit more milk or cream. If too thin, add more powdered sugar.

Lemon Raspberry Cake is a beautifully flavored dessert that offers a delightful combination of tart lemon and sweet raspberries. It's a refreshing choice for any celebration or as a special treat!

Blackberry Ginger Cake

Ingredients:

For the Cake:

- 1 1/2 cups (190g) all-purpose flour
- 1 1/2 teaspoons baking powder
- 1/2 teaspoon baking soda
- 1/4 teaspoon salt
- 1 teaspoon ground ginger
- 1/2 teaspoon ground cinnamon
- 1/4 teaspoon ground cloves
- 1/2 cup (115g) unsalted butter, softened
- 1 cup (200g) granulated sugar
- 2 large eggs
- 1/2 cup (120ml) buttermilk or milk
- 1/4 cup (60ml) fresh ginger syrup or molasses (for an extra kick of ginger flavor)
- 1 cup (150g) fresh blackberries (if using frozen, thaw and drain them)
- 1 tablespoon all-purpose flour (for tossing the blackberries)

For the Ginger Cream Cheese Frosting:

- 8 oz (225g) cream cheese, softened
- 1/2 cup (115g) unsalted butter, softened
- 2 cups (240g) powdered sugar
- 2 tablespoons fresh ginger syrup or molasses
- 1 teaspoon vanilla extract
- 1 teaspoon ground ginger (optional, for extra spice)

For Garnish (optional):

- Additional fresh blackberries
- Crystallized ginger pieces
- A dusting of powdered sugar

Instructions:

1. **Prepare the Cake:**
   - Preheat your oven to 350°F (175°C). Grease and flour a 9-inch (23cm) round cake pan or line it with parchment paper.
   - In a medium bowl, whisk together the flour, baking powder, baking soda, salt, ground ginger, cinnamon, and cloves. Set aside.
   - In a large bowl, cream together the softened butter and granulated sugar until light and fluffy.
   - Beat in the eggs one at a time, mixing well after each addition.

- Stir in the buttermilk and fresh ginger syrup or molasses until well combined.
- Gradually add the dry ingredients to the wet mixture, mixing until just combined.
- Toss the blackberries with 1 tablespoon of flour to coat them. Gently fold the coated blackberries into the batter.
- Pour the batter into the prepared cake pan and smooth the top with a spatula.

2. **Bake the Cake:**
    - Bake in the preheated oven for 30-35 minutes, or until a toothpick inserted into the center comes out clean and the cake is golden brown.
    - Allow the cake to cool in the pan for 10 minutes, then transfer to a wire rack to cool completely.

3. **Prepare the Ginger Cream Cheese Frosting:**
    - In a large bowl, beat the softened cream cheese and butter until creamy and smooth.
    - Gradually add the powdered sugar, mixing well after each addition.
    - Mix in the fresh ginger syrup or molasses and vanilla extract until well combined. If desired, add ground ginger for extra spice.
    - Adjust the consistency with more powdered sugar if needed.

4. **Assemble and Frost the Cake:**
    - Once the cake is completely cooled, place it on a serving plate or cake stand.
    - Spread a layer of ginger cream cheese frosting over the top and sides of the cake.
    - Garnish with additional fresh blackberries, crystallized ginger pieces, and a dusting of powdered sugar if desired.

5. **Serve:**
    - Slice and serve the cake at room temperature. It pairs wonderfully with a cup of tea or a light dessert wine.

Tips:

- **Blackberries:** Gently fold in the blackberries to avoid breaking them up too much. If using frozen blackberries, make sure to thaw and drain them thoroughly to prevent excess moisture in the batter.
- **Ginger Syrup:** If fresh ginger syrup is not available, you can use molasses as a substitute for a slightly different flavor profile.
- **Frosting Consistency:** If the frosting is too thick, add a little milk or cream to reach your desired consistency. If too thin, add more powdered sugar.

Blackberry Ginger Cake is a delightful dessert that combines the tartness of blackberries with the warm spice of ginger. It's sure to impress with its unique flavors and elegant presentation!

Poppy Seed Cake

Ingredients:

For the Cake:

- 1 1/2 cups (190g) all-purpose flour
- 1 1/2 teaspoons baking powder
- 1/2 teaspoon baking soda
- 1/4 teaspoon salt
- 1/2 cup (115g) unsalted butter, softened
- 1 cup (200g) granulated sugar
- 2 large eggs
- 1/2 cup (120ml) buttermilk or milk
- 1/4 cup (60ml) fresh lemon juice
- 1 tablespoon lemon zest (from about 1 lemon)
- 1/4 cup (30g) poppy seeds
- 1 teaspoon vanilla extract

For the Lemon Glaze (optional):

- 1 cup (120g) powdered sugar
- 2-3 tablespoons fresh lemon juice
- 1 teaspoon lemon zest

For Garnish (optional):

- Lemon zest
- Poppy seeds

Instructions:

1. **Prepare the Cake:**
    - Preheat your oven to 350°F (175°C). Grease and flour a 9-inch (23cm) round cake pan or line it with parchment paper.
    - In a medium bowl, whisk together the flour, baking powder, baking soda, and salt. Set aside.
    - In a large bowl, cream together the softened butter and granulated sugar until light and fluffy.
    - Beat in the eggs one at a time, mixing well after each addition.
    - Stir in the lemon juice, lemon zest, and vanilla extract.
    - Gradually add the dry ingredients to the wet mixture, alternating with the buttermilk (or milk). Begin and end with the flour mixture. Mix until just combined.
    - Fold in the poppy seeds.
    - Pour the batter into the prepared cake pan and smooth the top with a spatula.
2. **Bake the Cake:**

- Bake in the preheated oven for 25-30 minutes, or until a toothpick inserted into the center comes out clean and the cake is golden brown.
- Allow the cake to cool in the pan for 10 minutes, then transfer to a wire rack to cool completely.

3. **Prepare the Lemon Glaze (optional):**
    - In a small bowl, whisk together the powdered sugar, lemon juice, and lemon zest until smooth. Adjust the consistency with more lemon juice or powdered sugar as needed.
4. **Glaze the Cake (optional):**
    - Once the cake is completely cooled, drizzle the lemon glaze over the top. Let it set before slicing.
5. **Serve:**
    - Slice and serve the cake at room temperature. It pairs beautifully with a cup of tea or coffee.

Tips:

- **Poppy Seeds:** Toasting the poppy seeds lightly before adding them to the batter can enhance their flavor. Be careful not to burn them.
- **Lemon Juice:** For a more intense lemon flavor, you can use lemon extract in addition to the fresh lemon juice and zest.
- **Storage:** The cake can be stored in an airtight container at room temperature for up to 3 days. It can also be refrigerated for up to a week or frozen for up to 2 months.

Poppy Seed Cake is a simple yet elegant dessert with a delightful texture and flavor. It's perfect for any occasion, from casual gatherings to special celebrations!

Maple Berry Bundt Cake

Ingredients:

For the Cake:

- 2 1/2 cups (315g) all-purpose flour
- 1 1/2 teaspoons baking powder
- 1/2 teaspoon baking soda
- 1/4 teaspoon salt
- 1/2 cup (115g) unsalted butter, softened
- 1 cup (200g) granulated sugar
- 1/2 cup (120ml) pure maple syrup
- 1/4 cup (60ml) vegetable oil
- 3 large eggs
- 1 cup (240ml) buttermilk or milk
- 1 teaspoon vanilla extract
- 1 cup (150g) mixed fresh berries (such as blueberries, raspberries, and chopped strawberries) (if using frozen, thaw and drain them)
- 1 tablespoon all-purpose flour (for tossing the berries)

For the Maple Glaze:

- 1 cup (120g) powdered sugar
- 2-3 tablespoons pure maple syrup
- 1-2 tablespoons milk or cream (to adjust consistency)

For Garnish (optional):

- Additional fresh berries
- A dusting of powdered sugar

Instructions:

1. **Prepare the Cake:**
    - Preheat your oven to 350°F (175°C). Grease and flour a 10-cup bundt pan or spray it with non-stick baking spray.
    - In a medium bowl, whisk together the flour, baking powder, baking soda, and salt. Set aside.
    - In a large bowl, cream together the softened butter and granulated sugar until light and fluffy.
    - Mix in the maple syrup and vegetable oil until well combined.
    - Beat in the eggs one at a time, mixing well after each addition.
    - Stir in the vanilla extract.
    - Gradually add the dry ingredients to the wet mixture, alternating with the buttermilk (or milk). Begin and end with the flour mixture. Mix until just combined.

- Toss the fresh berries with 1 tablespoon of flour to coat them. Gently fold the coated berries into the batter.
- Pour the batter into the prepared bundt pan and smooth the top with a spatula.

2. **Bake the Cake:**
   - Bake in the preheated oven for 50-60 minutes, or until a toothpick inserted into the center comes out clean and the cake is golden brown.
   - Allow the cake to cool in the pan for 15 minutes, then carefully invert it onto a wire rack to cool completely.

3. **Prepare the Maple Glaze:**
   - In a small bowl, whisk together the powdered sugar, maple syrup, and milk or cream until smooth. Adjust the consistency with more milk or powdered sugar as needed.

4. **Glaze the Cake:**
   - Once the cake is completely cooled, drizzle the maple glaze over the top, allowing it to cascade down the sides of the cake.

5. **Serve:**
   - Garnish with additional fresh berries and a dusting of powdered sugar if desired. Slice and serve the cake at room temperature.

Tips:

- **Berries:** Gently fold in the berries to prevent them from breaking up too much. Coating them with flour helps to keep them from sinking to the bottom of the cake.
- **Maple Syrup:** Use pure maple syrup for the best flavor. Imitation maple syrup can be used in a pinch but may not provide the same depth of flavor.
- **Storage:** The cake can be stored in an airtight container at room temperature for up to 3 days. It can also be refrigerated for up to a week or frozen for up to 2 months.

Maple Berry Bundt Cake is a delightful combination of sweet maple and tangy berries, perfect for any time you want a cozy, indulgent treat. Enjoy!

Chocolate Chai Cake

Ingredients:

For the Cake:

- 1 1/2 cups (190g) all-purpose flour
- 1 cup (200g) granulated sugar
- 1/2 cup (50g) unsweetened cocoa powder
- 1 1/2 teaspoons baking powder
- 1 teaspoon baking soda
- 1/2 teaspoon salt
- 1 teaspoon ground cinnamon
- 1/2 teaspoon ground ginger
- 1/2 teaspoon ground cardamom
- 1/4 teaspoon ground cloves
- 1/4 teaspoon black pepper
- 1/2 cup (115g) unsalted butter, softened
- 2 large eggs
- 1 cup (240ml) brewed chai tea (cooled)
- 1/2 cup (120ml) milk
- 1 teaspoon vanilla extract

For the Chai Spice Buttercream Frosting:

- 1/2 cup (115g) unsalted butter, softened
- 2 cups (240g) powdered sugar
- 2 tablespoons brewed chai tea (cooled)
- 1 tablespoon milk or cream (if needed for consistency)
- 1 teaspoon ground cinnamon
- 1/2 teaspoon ground ginger
- 1/2 teaspoon ground cardamom

For Garnish (optional):

- Shaved chocolate
- A sprinkle of chai spice mix (cinnamon, ginger, cardamom)

Instructions:

1. **Prepare the Cake:**
    - Preheat your oven to 350°F (175°C). Grease and flour two 8-inch (20cm) round cake pans or line them with parchment paper.
    - In a medium bowl, whisk together the flour, granulated sugar, cocoa powder, baking powder, baking soda, salt, cinnamon, ginger, cardamom, cloves, and black pepper. Set aside.

- In a large bowl, cream together the softened butter and sugar until light and fluffy.
- Beat in the eggs one at a time, mixing well after each addition.
- Stir in the vanilla extract.
- Gradually add the dry ingredients to the wet mixture, alternating with the brewed chai tea and milk. Begin and end with the dry ingredients. Mix until just combined.
- Divide the batter evenly between the prepared cake pans and smooth the tops with a spatula.

2. **Bake the Cake:**
   - Bake in the preheated oven for 25-30 minutes, or until a toothpick inserted into the center comes out clean and the cakes are set.
   - Allow the cakes to cool in the pans for 10 minutes, then transfer to a wire rack to cool completely.

3. **Prepare the Chai Spice Buttercream Frosting:**
   - In a large bowl, beat the softened butter until creamy.
   - Gradually add the powdered sugar, mixing well after each addition.
   - Mix in the brewed chai tea, milk or cream, cinnamon, ginger, and cardamom until the frosting is smooth and fluffy.

4. **Assemble and Frost the Cake:**
   - Once the cakes are completely cooled, place one layer on a serving plate or cake stand.
   - Spread a layer of chai spice buttercream frosting over the top.
   - Place the second layer on top and frost the top and sides of the cake with the remaining frosting.
   - Garnish with shaved chocolate and a sprinkle of chai spice mix if desired.

5. **Serve:**
   - Slice and serve the cake at room temperature. It pairs wonderfully with a cup of chai tea or coffee.

Tips:

- **Chai Tea:** Use a strong brewed chai tea for the best flavor. You can make your own chai tea blend or use a store-bought chai tea bag.
- **Spices:** Adjust the spices according to your preference. If you prefer a spicier cake, you can increase the amounts of cinnamon, ginger, cardamom, or cloves.
- **Frosting Consistency:** If the frosting is too thick, add a bit more milk or cream. If too thin, add more powdered sugar to achieve your desired consistency.

Chocolate Chai Cake is a comforting and indulgent dessert that beautifully combines the richness of chocolate with the aromatic spices of chai. It's perfect for a cozy afternoon treat or a special celebration!

Fig and Walnut Cake

Ingredients:

For the Cake:

- 1 1/2 cups (190g) all-purpose flour
- 1 teaspoon baking powder
- 1/2 teaspoon baking soda
- 1/4 teaspoon salt
- 1 teaspoon ground cinnamon
- 1/2 teaspoon ground nutmeg
- 1/2 cup (115g) unsalted butter, softened
- 1 cup (200g) granulated sugar
- 2 large eggs
- 1 cup (240ml) buttermilk or milk
- 1 teaspoon vanilla extract
- 1 cup (150g) dried figs, chopped
- 1/2 cup (60g) walnuts, chopped (plus extra for garnish, if desired)

For the Cream Cheese Frosting (optional):

- 8 oz (225g) cream cheese, softened
- 1/2 cup (115g) unsalted butter, softened
- 2 cups (240g) powdered sugar
- 1 teaspoon vanilla extract
- 1-2 tablespoons milk or cream (if needed for consistency)

For Garnish (optional):

- Extra chopped walnuts
- Fresh figs (if in season)
- A dusting of powdered sugar

Instructions:

1. **Prepare the Cake:**
    - Preheat your oven to 350°F (175°C). Grease and flour a 9-inch (23cm) round cake pan or line it with parchment paper.
    - In a medium bowl, whisk together the flour, baking powder, baking soda, salt, cinnamon, and nutmeg. Set aside.
    - In a large bowl, cream together the softened butter and granulated sugar until light and fluffy.
    - Beat in the eggs one at a time, mixing well after each addition.
    - Stir in the vanilla extract.

- Gradually add the dry ingredients to the wet mixture, alternating with the buttermilk (or milk). Begin and end with the dry ingredients. Mix until just combined.
- Gently fold in the chopped figs and walnuts.
- Pour the batter into the prepared cake pan and smooth the top with a spatula.

2. **Bake the Cake:**
   - Bake in the preheated oven for 30-35 minutes, or until a toothpick inserted into the center comes out clean and the cake is golden brown.
   - Allow the cake to cool in the pan for 10 minutes, then transfer to a wire rack to cool completely.
3. **Prepare the Cream Cheese Frosting (optional):**
   - In a large bowl, beat the softened cream cheese and butter until creamy and smooth.
   - Gradually add the powdered sugar, mixing well after each addition.
   - Mix in the vanilla extract. If the frosting is too thick, add milk or cream a little at a time until the desired consistency is reached.
4. **Assemble and Frost the Cake (optional):**
   - Once the cake is completely cooled, place it on a serving plate or cake stand.
   - Spread a layer of cream cheese frosting over the top and sides of the cake.
   - Garnish with extra chopped walnuts, fresh figs (if in season), and a dusting of powdered sugar if desired.
5. **Serve:**
   - Slice and serve the cake at room temperature. It pairs wonderfully with a cup of tea or coffee.

Tips:

- **Figs:** If the dried figs are very dry, you can soak them in warm water for about 15 minutes to soften them before chopping.
- **Walnuts:** Toasting the walnuts lightly before adding them to the batter can enhance their flavor. Be careful not to burn them.
- **Frosting Consistency:** If you prefer a thicker or thinner frosting, adjust the amount of milk or cream as needed.

Fig and Walnut Cake is a delightful dessert that combines the rich flavors of figs and walnuts in a moist and satisfying cake. Whether enjoyed plain or with a creamy frosting, it's sure to be a hit with family and friends!

Vanilla Bean Cake

Ingredients:

For the Cake:

- 2 1/2 cups (315g) all-purpose flour
- 2 teaspoons baking powder
- 1/2 teaspoon baking soda
- 1/4 teaspoon salt
- 1 cup (230g) unsalted butter, softened
- 1 1/2 cups (300g) granulated sugar
- 4 large eggs
- 1 cup (240ml) buttermilk or whole milk
- 1 tablespoon vanilla bean paste (or 1-2 vanilla beans, scraped)
- 1 teaspoon vanilla extract

For the Vanilla Bean Buttercream Frosting:

- 1 cup (230g) unsalted butter, softened
- 3-4 cups (360-480g) powdered sugar (adjust to desired sweetness)
- 2-3 tablespoons heavy cream or milk (adjust for consistency)
- 1 tablespoon vanilla bean paste (or 1-2 vanilla beans, scraped)
- 1 teaspoon vanilla extract

For Garnish (optional):

- Additional vanilla beans
- Fresh berries or edible flowers

Instructions:

1. **Prepare the Cake:**
    - Preheat your oven to 350°F (175°C). Grease and flour two 8-inch (20cm) round cake pans or line them with parchment paper.
    - In a medium bowl, whisk together the flour, baking powder, baking soda, and salt. Set aside.
    - In a large bowl, cream together the softened butter and granulated sugar until light and fluffy.
    - Beat in the eggs one at a time, mixing well after each addition.
    - Stir in the vanilla bean paste (or scraped vanilla beans) and vanilla extract.
    - Gradually add the dry ingredients to the wet mixture, alternating with the buttermilk (or milk). Begin and end with the dry ingredients. Mix until just combined.
    - Divide the batter evenly between the prepared cake pans and smooth the tops with a spatula.

2. **Bake the Cake:**
    - Bake in the preheated oven for 25-30 minutes, or until a toothpick inserted into the center comes out clean and the cakes are golden brown.
    - Allow the cakes to cool in the pans for 10 minutes, then transfer to a wire rack to cool completely.
3. **Prepare the Vanilla Bean Buttercream Frosting:**
    - In a large bowl, beat the softened butter until creamy.
    - Gradually add the powdered sugar, mixing well after each addition.
    - Mix in the vanilla bean paste (or scraped vanilla beans) and vanilla extract.
    - Add heavy cream or milk, one tablespoon at a time, until the frosting reaches your desired consistency.
4. **Assemble and Frost the Cake:**
    - Once the cakes are completely cooled, place one layer on a serving plate or cake stand.
    - Spread a layer of vanilla bean buttercream frosting over the top.
    - Place the second layer on top and frost the top and sides of the cake with the remaining buttercream.
    - Garnish with additional vanilla beans, fresh berries, or edible flowers if desired.
5. **Serve:**
    - Slice and serve the cake at room temperature. It pairs beautifully with a cup of coffee or tea.

Tips:

- **Vanilla Beans vs. Vanilla Bean Paste:** Vanilla bean paste provides a more intense flavor and is easier to use compared to whole vanilla beans. If using vanilla beans, make sure to scrape out the seeds and add them to the batter and frosting.
- **Butter Temperature:** Ensure the butter is softened but not melted. This will help create a smooth and creamy batter and frosting.
- **Frosting Consistency:** Adjust the amount of powdered sugar and heavy cream or milk to achieve the desired consistency of the frosting.

Vanilla Bean Cake is a timeless classic that highlights the beauty and simplicity of vanilla. Its rich flavor and elegant appearance make it a perfect choice for any occasion!

Huckleberry Cake

Ingredients:

For the Cake:

- 1 1/2 cups (190g) all-purpose flour
- 1 1/2 teaspoons baking powder
- 1/2 teaspoon baking soda
- 1/4 teaspoon salt
- 1/2 teaspoon ground cinnamon (optional)
- 1/2 cup (115g) unsalted butter, softened
- 1 cup (200g) granulated sugar
- 2 large eggs
- 1 teaspoon vanilla extract
- 1 cup (240ml) buttermilk or milk
- 1 1/2 cups (225g) fresh or frozen huckleberries (if using frozen, do not thaw)
- 1 tablespoon all-purpose flour (for tossing the huckleberries)

For the Glaze (optional):

- 1 cup (120g) powdered sugar
- 2-3 tablespoons lemon juice (adjust for consistency)
- 1 teaspoon lemon zest (optional)

For Garnish (optional):

- Additional huckleberries
- Lemon zest
- Fresh mint leaves

Instructions:

1. **Prepare the Cake:**
    - Preheat your oven to 350°F (175°C). Grease and flour a 9-inch (23cm) round cake pan or line it with parchment paper.
    - In a medium bowl, whisk together the flour, baking powder, baking soda, salt, and cinnamon (if using). Set aside.
    - In a large bowl, cream together the softened butter and granulated sugar until light and fluffy.
    - Beat in the eggs one at a time, mixing well after each addition.
    - Stir in the vanilla extract.
    - Gradually add the dry ingredients to the wet mixture, alternating with the buttermilk (or milk). Begin and end with the dry ingredients. Mix until just combined.

- Toss the huckleberries with 1 tablespoon of flour to coat them. Gently fold the coated huckleberries into the batter.
- Pour the batter into the prepared cake pan and smooth the top with a spatula.

2. **Bake the Cake:**
   - Bake in the preheated oven for 30-35 minutes, or until a toothpick inserted into the center comes out clean and the cake is golden brown.
   - Allow the cake to cool in the pan for 10 minutes, then transfer to a wire rack to cool completely.
3. **Prepare the Glaze (optional):**
   - In a small bowl, whisk together the powdered sugar and lemon juice until smooth. Adjust the consistency with more lemon juice or powdered sugar as needed. Mix in lemon zest if desired.
4. **Glaze the Cake (optional):**
   - Once the cake is completely cooled, drizzle the glaze over the top. Allow the glaze to set before slicing.
5. **Serve:**
   - Garnish with additional huckleberries, lemon zest, and fresh mint leaves if desired. Slice and serve the cake at room temperature.

Tips:

- **Huckleberries:** If fresh huckleberries are not available, you can use frozen huckleberries. Just be sure to toss them with flour to prevent them from sinking to the bottom of the cake.
- **Flour:** Tossing the huckleberries in flour helps to distribute them evenly throughout the batter.
- **Storage:** The cake can be stored in an airtight container at room temperature for up to 3 days or refrigerated for up to a week. It can also be frozen for up to 2 months.

Huckleberry Cake is a delicious and unique dessert that celebrates the distinct flavor of huckleberries. Its moist texture and fruity taste make it a wonderful treat for any occasion!

Maple Bacon Caramel Cake

Ingredients:

For the Cake:

- 2 1/2 cups (315g) all-purpose flour
- 1 1/2 teaspoons baking powder
- 1/2 teaspoon baking soda
- 1/4 teaspoon salt
- 1 cup (230g) unsalted butter, softened
- 1 cup (200g) granulated sugar
- 1/2 cup (100g) brown sugar, packed
- 3 large eggs
- 1 cup (240ml) pure maple syrup
- 1 cup (240ml) buttermilk or milk
- 1 teaspoon vanilla extract
- 1/2 cup (60g) crispy bacon bits (from about 6-8 strips of bacon, cooked and crumbled)

For the Caramel Frosting:

- 1 cup (230g) unsalted butter, softened
- 2 cups (240g) powdered sugar
- 1/2 cup (120ml) homemade or store-bought caramel sauce (plus extra for drizzling)
- 2 tablespoons heavy cream or milk (adjust for consistency)
- 1 teaspoon vanilla extract

For Garnish:

- Extra crispy bacon bits
- Caramel sauce
- A pinch of sea salt (optional)

Instructions:

1. **Prepare the Cake:**
    - Preheat your oven to 350°F (175°C). Grease and flour two 8-inch (20cm) round cake pans or line them with parchment paper.
    - In a medium bowl, whisk together the flour, baking powder, baking soda, and salt. Set aside.
    - In a large bowl, cream together the softened butter, granulated sugar, and brown sugar until light and fluffy.
    - Beat in the eggs one at a time, mixing well after each addition.
    - Stir in the maple syrup, vanilla extract, and buttermilk (or milk).
    - Gradually add the dry ingredients to the wet mixture, mixing until just combined.
    - Gently fold in the crispy bacon bits.

- Divide the batter evenly between the prepared cake pans and smooth the tops with a spatula.
2. **Bake the Cake:**
    - Bake in the preheated oven for 30-35 minutes, or until a toothpick inserted into the center comes out clean and the cakes are golden brown.
    - Allow the cakes to cool in the pans for 10 minutes, then transfer to a wire rack to cool completely.
3. **Prepare the Caramel Frosting:**
    - In a large bowl, beat the softened butter until creamy.
    - Gradually add the powdered sugar, mixing well after each addition.
    - Mix in the caramel sauce, vanilla extract, and heavy cream or milk. Continue to beat until the frosting is smooth and fluffy.
4. **Assemble and Frost the Cake:**
    - Once the cakes are completely cooled, place one layer on a serving plate or cake stand.
    - Spread a layer of caramel frosting over the top.
    - Place the second layer on top and frost the top and sides of the cake with the remaining caramel frosting.
    - Drizzle extra caramel sauce over the top and sprinkle with additional crispy bacon bits. Optionally, add a pinch of sea salt for a touch of contrast.
5. **Serve:**
    - Slice and serve the cake at room temperature. Enjoy with a cup of coffee or tea.

Tips:

- **Bacon:** For best results, cook the bacon until crispy and crumble it into small bits. You can cook the bacon in advance and store it in an airtight container until ready to use.
- **Caramel Sauce:** Use homemade or high-quality store-bought caramel sauce for the best flavor. You can make your own by cooking sugar and cream together until it thickens.
- **Frosting Consistency:** Adjust the amount of heavy cream or milk to achieve your desired frosting consistency.

Maple Bacon Caramel Cake is a unique and indulgent treat that brings together sweet and savory flavors in a deliciously satisfying way. It's perfect for special occasions or whenever you want to impress with a creative dessert!

Chocolate Cherry Cake

Ingredients:

For the Cake:

- 1 3/4 cups (220g) all-purpose flour
- 1 1/2 teaspoons baking powder
- 1 teaspoon baking soda
- 1/2 teaspoon salt
- 1/2 cup (50g) unsweetened cocoa powder
- 1 cup (200g) granulated sugar
- 1/2 cup (100g) brown sugar, packed
- 1/2 cup (115g) unsalted butter, softened
- 2 large eggs
- 1 cup (240ml) buttermilk or whole milk
- 1 teaspoon vanilla extract
- 1 cup (225g) fresh or frozen cherries, pitted and chopped (if using frozen, do not thaw)
- 1 tablespoon all-purpose flour (for tossing the cherries)

For the Cherry Filling (optional):

- 1 cup (225g) fresh or frozen cherries, pitted and chopped
- 1/4 cup (50g) granulated sugar
- 1 tablespoon cornstarch
- 1 tablespoon water or cherry juice

For the Chocolate Frosting:

- 1 cup (230g) unsalted butter, softened
- 2 cups (240g) powdered sugar
- 1/2 cup (50g) unsweetened cocoa powder
- 1/4 cup (60ml) heavy cream or milk
- 1 teaspoon vanilla extract
- A pinch of salt

For Garnish (optional):

- Additional fresh cherries
- Chocolate shavings or curls
- A sprinkle of powdered sugar

Instructions:

1. **Prepare the Cake:**

- Preheat your oven to 350°F (175°C). Grease and flour two 8-inch (20cm) round cake pans or line them with parchment paper.
- In a medium bowl, whisk together the flour, baking powder, baking soda, salt, and cocoa powder. Set aside.
- In a large bowl, cream together the softened butter, granulated sugar, and brown sugar until light and fluffy.
- Beat in the eggs one at a time, mixing well after each addition.
- Stir in the vanilla extract.
- Gradually add the dry ingredients to the wet mixture, alternating with the buttermilk (or milk). Begin and end with the dry ingredients. Mix until just combined.
- Toss the chopped cherries with 1 tablespoon of flour to coat them. Gently fold the cherries into the batter.
- Divide the batter evenly between the prepared cake pans and smooth the tops with a spatula.

2. **Bake the Cake:**
    - Bake in the preheated oven for 25-30 minutes, or until a toothpick inserted into the center comes out clean and the cakes are set.
    - Allow the cakes to cool in the pans for 10 minutes, then transfer to a wire rack to cool completely.

3. **Prepare the Cherry Filling (optional):**
    - In a small saucepan, combine the cherries, granulated sugar, cornstarch, and water or cherry juice.
    - Cook over medium heat, stirring frequently, until the mixture thickens and becomes syrupy. Remove from heat and let cool.

4. **Prepare the Chocolate Frosting:**
    - In a large bowl, beat the softened butter until creamy.
    - Gradually add the powdered sugar and cocoa powder, mixing well after each addition.
    - Mix in the heavy cream or milk, vanilla extract, and a pinch of salt. Continue to beat until the frosting is smooth and fluffy.

5. **Assemble and Frost the Cake:**
    - Once the cakes are completely cooled, place one layer on a serving plate or cake stand.
    - If using the cherry filling, spread a layer of cherry filling over the top of the first cake layer.
    - Place the second layer on top and frost the top and sides of the cake with the chocolate frosting.
    - Garnish with additional fresh cherries, chocolate shavings or curls, and a sprinkle of powdered sugar if desired.

6. **Serve:**
    - Slice and serve the cake at room temperature. It pairs beautifully with a glass of milk or a cup of coffee.

Tips:

- **Cherries:** If fresh cherries are not available, you can use canned cherries, but be sure to drain them well. If using frozen cherries, do not thaw them before adding to the batter.
- **Frosting Consistency:** Adjust the amount of heavy cream or milk to achieve your desired frosting consistency. Add more powdered sugar if the frosting is too thin.
- **Storage:** Store the cake in an airtight container at room temperature for up to 3 days, or refrigerate for up to a week. The cake can also be frozen for up to 2 months.

Chocolate Cherry Cake is a delicious treat that combines rich chocolate with the bright, fruity flavor of cherries. It's a perfect dessert for any celebration or a sweet indulgence for any day!

Butternut Squash Cake

Ingredients:

For the Cake:

- 2 cups (250g) all-purpose flour
- 1 1/2 teaspoons baking powder
- 1 teaspoon baking soda
- 1/2 teaspoon salt
- 1 teaspoon ground cinnamon
- 1/2 teaspoon ground nutmeg
- 1/2 teaspoon ground ginger
- 1/4 teaspoon ground cloves
- 1/2 cup (115g) unsalted butter, softened
- 1 cup (200g) granulated sugar
- 1/2 cup (100g) packed brown sugar
- 3 large eggs
- 1 cup (240ml) buttermilk or whole milk
- 1 cup (225g) cooked butternut squash, mashed and cooled (about 1 small butternut squash)
- 1 teaspoon vanilla extract

For the Cream Cheese Frosting (optional):

- 1/2 cup (115g) unsalted butter, softened
- 8 oz (225g) cream cheese, softened
- 4 cups (480g) powdered sugar
- 1 teaspoon vanilla extract
- A pinch of salt

For Garnish (optional):

- Toasted nuts (e.g., pecans or walnuts)
- Ground cinnamon
- Fresh mint leaves

Instructions:

1. **Prepare the Butternut Squash:**
    - Preheat your oven to 400°F (200°C). Cut the butternut squash in half, remove the seeds, and place the halves cut-side down on a baking sheet.
    - Roast in the preheated oven for 45-60 minutes, or until tender. Let it cool, then scoop out the flesh and mash it until smooth. Measure out 1 cup of mashed butternut squash.
2. **Prepare the Cake:**

- Preheat your oven to 350°F (175°C). Grease and flour two 8-inch (20cm) round cake pans or line them with parchment paper.
- In a medium bowl, whisk together the flour, baking powder, baking soda, salt, cinnamon, nutmeg, ginger, and cloves. Set aside.
- In a large bowl, cream together the softened butter, granulated sugar, and brown sugar until light and fluffy.
- Beat in the eggs one at a time, mixing well after each addition.
- Stir in the vanilla extract and mashed butternut squash.
- Gradually add the dry ingredients to the wet mixture, alternating with the buttermilk (or milk). Begin and end with the dry ingredients. Mix until just combined.
- Divide the batter evenly between the prepared cake pans and smooth the tops with a spatula.

3. **Bake the Cake:**
   - Bake in the preheated oven for 25-30 minutes, or until a toothpick inserted into the center comes out clean and the cakes are golden brown.
   - Allow the cakes to cool in the pans for 10 minutes, then transfer to a wire rack to cool completely.

4. **Prepare the Cream Cheese Frosting (optional):**
   - In a large bowl, beat the softened butter and cream cheese together until smooth and creamy.
   - Gradually add the powdered sugar, mixing well after each addition.
   - Mix in the vanilla extract and a pinch of salt. Beat until the frosting is smooth and fluffy.

5. **Assemble and Frost the Cake:**
   - Once the cakes are completely cooled, place one layer on a serving plate or cake stand.
   - Spread a layer of cream cheese frosting over the top.
   - Place the second layer on top and frost the top and sides of the cake with the remaining cream cheese frosting.
   - Garnish with toasted nuts, a sprinkle of ground cinnamon, and fresh mint leaves if desired.

6. **Serve:**
   - Slice and serve the cake at room temperature. It pairs wonderfully with a cup of tea or coffee.

Tips:

- **Butternut Squash:** You can use canned butternut squash puree if you prefer, but homemade puree will give a fresher taste. Just be sure to drain any excess liquid.
- **Spices:** Adjust the spices to your taste or try adding a pinch of ground allspice for extra warmth.
- **Storage:** The cake can be stored in an airtight container at room temperature for up to 3 days, or refrigerated for up to a week. It can also be frozen for up to 2 months.

Butternut Squash Cake is a comforting and delicious treat that highlights the natural sweetness of butternut squash. Its warm spices and creamy frosting make it a delightful dessert for any occasion!

www.ingramcontent.com/pod-product-compliance
Lightning Source LLC
LaVergne TN
LVHW081555060526
838201LV00054B/1906